Artiste   Roger Eno
Title   Between Tides
Rec Co   Land
Date   1988
Design   & Artwork Russell Mills and Dave Coppenhall; Cover Russell Mills

COMPILED BY ROGER DEAN, STORM THORGERSON AND NIGEL GRIERSON

A Dragon's World Imprint
Dragon's World Ltd
Limpsfield
Surrey RH8 0DY
Great Britain

First published by Paper Tiger Books, an
imprint of Dragon's World, 1989.
© Dragon's World 1989
© Roger Dean & Storm Thorgerson 1989
© Logo, Roger Dean 1977, 1982, 1984, 1987,
    1989

**British Library Cataloging in Publication
Data**

Album cover album.
5.
1. Sound discs. Sleeves, 1970-1987
I. Dean, Roger, 1944-
796.5

ISBN Hardback 1 85028 076 2
        Limpback 1 85028 077 0

Typeset by The Works, Exeter, Devon.

Printed in Singapore

CONTENTS

ACKNOWLEDGMENTS

We have had a great deal of help from designers and record companies. In particular we would thank all the following:

All the staff at Virgin Records Megastore, Brighton; Adrian Halkes; Linda Cobb; Julia Matchett; Lothar Mattejat; Alex (EG Records); Linda Adams; Colin Miles; Tracey (Factory Records); Paul White; Casey Cashman; Mark Farrow; Gary Wathen; Amy Strauss; Mike Doud; Paul Maxon; Henry Marquez; Chris Austopchuk; Ria Lewerke; Paul McGarvey; John Warwicker; Rob O'Connor; Jane Manley; Luke Thornton; Liz Silver; Colin Chambers; Andrew Ellis; Keith Breeden; Malcolm Garrett

INTRODUCTION

Who reads Introductions anyway? Sometimes I think the Introduction is a leftover from the Victorian Age when publishers thought its formality a necessary and desirable courtesy. Then again the Introduction could be a ploy used by modern publishers as an inexpensive way to eat up pages — you know, make the book feel fatter and therefore more value for money. Either way, dear reader, please stay with me as I make a literal stab at it.

Herewith a marvellous book, brimful of exciting images and exquisite designs. It is called *Album Cover Album* because that's precisely what it is — an album, as in photo album, of record, or album, covers. It is a collection of what we consider to be the best record cover design during the last two years, since the appearance of *ACA 4* in 1988. And this is how we go about it.

Album covers are solicited from many record companies, care of their art directors (thanks very much, guys) both from the United States and Europe, and some from Japan and Hong Kong. Covers are also submitted by designers themselves, once we have bothered them a few times (and thanks, too, guys) and some are selected from private collections and from exhaustive visits to large record shops. We end up with approximately 2000 covers and their inner sleeves. These are preselected because all the material from art directors and designers is what they consider most appropriate. They don't send us just any old thing (at least I hope not).

This gives us about 4 to 5000 designs all told including back covers, liner bags, singles, etc. The actual covers are placed all around a large room and discussed vigorously by your humble editors. Firstly we go through all of them, eliminating those the three of us clearly don't like. Then there is a 'maybe' pile and a 'definites' pile. The definites require two 'yesses' and the maybes at least one 'yes'. Are you still with me dear reader? Then the definites are divided into single page (three 'yesses') or four on a page. If we run out of definites to fill the pages in the book we raid the maybe pile, paying particular attention then to how the designs fit together. Designers did not intend their work to be seen alongside other designs in such intimacy, but unless we arrange it like this we leave out too many good pieces. If we were to select one to a page we'd have a book that weighs a ton and cost a proverbial arm and a leg.

Suffice to say that we try our level best to arrange disparate covers sympathetically, or occasionally in direct juxtaposition, so that each design appears to its advantage. In similar vein, we try not to over-design the book at all, making the layout as minimal as possible — this is because there are supposed to be hundreds of carefully worked designs already in there.

The criterion used in selection is basically simple — it's what we consider good. This 'we' comprises two old but learned gents, Mr Roger Dean (Yes, Osibisa, Asia) and Mr Storm Thorgerson (Pink Floyd, Led Zeppelin). We welcome Mr Nigel Grierson (Modern English, Cocteau Twins, David Sylvian) to the fray as a representative of the younger fraternity. Now this sense of what's good is rather complex and private. It includes breadth of vision, innovation of approach or style, attention to detail, sympathy of graphics and image, nature of content, extent of humour etc. etc., or any combination of these values plus others not mentioned (ironically the only criterion not employed was the relation of the design to the music — there is no music with this book). The three editors have very different ideas about what is good, and consequently argued vociferously during selection. The contents of *ACA 5* constitute therefore a synthesis of these views, and

contain the best of what we could find. We trust you approve. Not totally of course, but for the main part. We are not greedy.

A few covers have been included as examples of type of approach (some portraits in particular), or very occasionally because they fitted a page of four really well. Some work is included to indicate certain trends, one example of which is design continuity. We have included it as Part Five in this present volume but will explore it more deeply in *ACA 6*. Seeing the packaging as a whole continues as top priority for some designers and they will therefore expand, develop and interrelate the work throughout the album, front and back, the inner sleeve, labels, and the singles which have been taken from the album. This holistic approach to record packaging can be seen in John Warwicker's work for Black (page 129) or Keith Breeden's work for ABC (page 127) but there are many other examples. In some cases a whole label develops a style, such as the Venture label by Icon (page 126), or a series for one artiste like Miles Davis (page 125). Different albums and singles may bear the design continuity, such as Scritti Politti (page 134-5), in much the same way as the music of any one artiste interrelates. Another example is the Oldland

Montano which is a sequence of photos on different faces of a three-pannelled single bag. Designers are only endeavouring to reflect the wholeness of the music.

Another trend is towards the textural or painterly approach and away from hard edge photography (Part Four). The image is less recognizable, the content less important − rather the feeling or the (decorative) form becomes more persuasive. Such work as Vaughan Oliver's Throwing Muses (page 117), or Steve Byram's Watusis (page 113), or Russell Mills' Between Tides (frontispiece). The photography becomes noticeably more abstract (page 121) or more impressionistic (as on page 115). In addition the graphics may become more integrated, less obtrusive, or just really small, unlike the usual record company marketing trend of big letters for the name of the band. This is a welcome move (for these editors) insomuch as it treats the design like the music − the punter can explore the design in the same way as he can explore the music.

Records are individually different, made much more so than hair sprays or refrigerators, and a lot more ozone friendly. So individual, in fact, that a German outfit called Trasch Center ALTONA inspired by

Artiste   Oldland Montano
Title   Sugar Mummy
Rec Co   Siren
Date   1987
Design   Michael Nash Assoc; Photog Andrew MacPherson

Lothar Mattejat, decided to hand-make all the covers of their albums. We show you only one here and it is sculptured, you can feel (well, you can't, dear reader, but we could) the ridges in the cut out cardboard windows. They hired 59 artists to hand-make 1000 covers. And each one is completely different! It makes you think... some people will go to extraordinary lengths.

And some will not. One of the few areas of disappointment in the field of 'Album Art' (as they call it in America) is the unbridled use of found pictures. Paintings, prints, photos are borrowed from all kinds of sources such as libraries, books and magazines. Sometimes it is hard to tell whether the album cover is stolen or not, like the Durutti Column (page 67) or Cassell Webb (page 110). In both cases we have included them because they are deployed tastefully. But the use of plagiarized material does not do a lot to

infuse the field of album design with innovation or originality, especially if used as in Fairground Attraction (page 22), as opposed to using it with imagination as in Gaye Bykers (page 25), or How We Live (page 18).

One other old chestnut I'd like to crack is the vexed and pompous issue of whether record packing is really art — or is any packaging for that matter. Part of me responds with a dismissive shrug of the shoulders — call it what you like, I got to go dancing. Another part responds quite violently, particularly to the insinuation that album covers are like all packaging and not good or serious enough to merit the description. Cover design is simply not the same as the majority of packaging which is dull, utilitarian, unimaginative and not art. Though most cornflakes I've eaten are the same, most music I've heard is very different. It is highly individualistic and idiosyncratic. Even the same group will make different records. And the record packaging is consequently very different, and in being different becomes imaginative and special. It is when it becomes special that it becomes art. It is a question of quality not of function. The relation between album design and art is straightforward — the best design is, the worst isn't.

Last but not least I had thought I might write a personal lament. You know the kind of thing: been in the business for 20 years and things just not the same any more, not as good as they used to be. Well I might have hoped I could do this, but I can't. The world of album cover design is alive and very kicking. This book contains some wonderful material — great stuff from the likes of Steve Byram, Russell Mills, Vaughan Oliver and Chris Austopchuk, from record companies like Land Records, 4AD, Virgin, CBS (NY) and from groups like Throwing Muses and the Art of Noise. Not to mention Martini Ranch. (I told you not to mention Martini Ranch).

Artiste   Gard Banker
Title   20 Trasch Center Hits
Rec Co   Drome & Trasch Center
Date   1988
Design   Gard Banker & Lothar Mattejat

PART ONE
GENERAL

This book is full of richness. Each cover has been lovingly designed, executed with care, and infused with thought. Sometimes there are four covers to a page. So we thought we would break up this unremitting brilliance into various chapters, and this division into parts came quite easily from the preferred material.

Part One is a general selection of some of the great cover designs from the last two or three years. It has no particular theme, rather it was what was left over when we had made the other sections more definite. The main things to note are the overall excellence and the great variety of different techniques used. Collage and montage (pages 18, 51), humour (37), psychedelic (36), paintings (20, 54), textural photography (49), hard-edged photography (43), black and white photography (22), illustration (30), and the bizarre (47). Album cover art is eclectic, if nothing else.

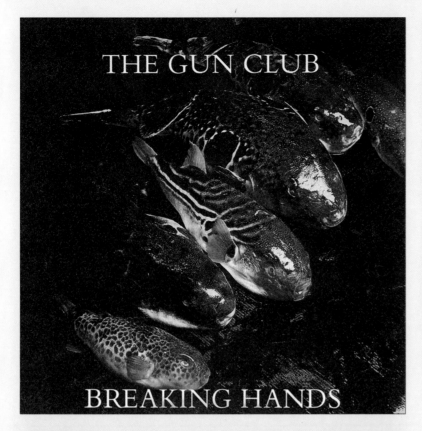

Artiste	The Gun Club
Title	Breaking Hands
Rec Co	Red Rhino
Date	1988
Design	–

Artiste	The Wolfgang Press
Title	Big Sex
Rec Co	4AD
Date	1987
Design	The Wolfgang Press & Vaughan Oliver

Artiste	Automatic Dlamini
Title	Me and My Conscience
Rec Co	Idea
Date	1987
Design	Photog Rob Ellis

Artiste	Howard Jones
Title	Life in One Day
Rec Co	WEA/Warner
Date	1985
Design	Rob O'Connor/Stylorouge; Photog Simon Fowler/Panni Charrington

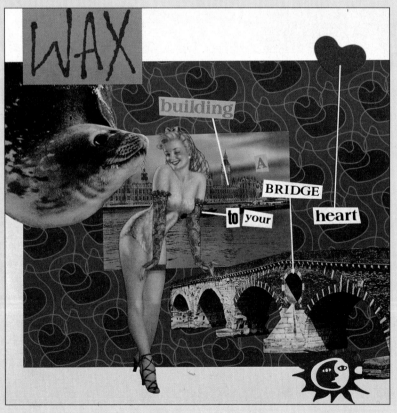

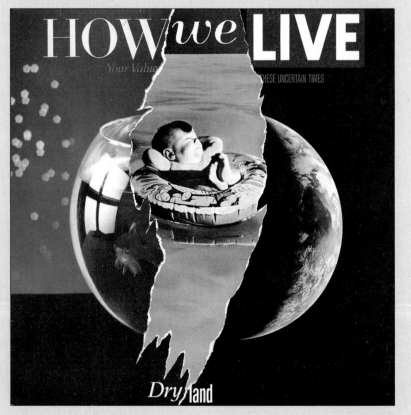

Artiste   Martini Ranch
Title   Reach
Rec Co   Sire
Date   1988
Design   Laura LiPuma; Photog Chris Cuffaro; Collage Art Lou Beach

Artiste   Wax
Title   Bridge to Your Heart
Rec Co   RCA
Date   1987
Design   & Art Dir Storm Thorgerson/Nexus; Artwork John F. McGill

Artiste   Herb Robertson Brass Ensemble
Title   Shades of Bud Powell
Rec Co   JMT/Polydor
Date   1988
Design   & Art Steve Byram

Artiste   How We Live
Title   Dry Land
Rec Co   Portrait/CBS
Date   1987
Design   Mike Ross

throwing muses • dizzy

Artiste   Throwing Muses
Title   Dizzy
Rec Co   4AD
Date   1989
Design   & Illus Vaughan Oliver/v23

Artiste   Oregon
Title   45th Parallel
Rec Co   CBS
Date   1989
Design   Art Dir Christopher Austopchuk; Illus Robert Coto

Artiste   Talking Heads
Title   Little Creatures
Rec Co   Sire
Date   1985
Design   Cover Painting Rev. Howard Finster; Design M & Co

Artiste   Living Colour
Title   Middleman
Rec Co   Epic/CBS
Date   1988
Design   The Thunderjockeys/Vivid I.D.

Artiste   Prefab Sprout
Title   Nightingales (12″)
Rec Co   Kitchenware/CBS
Date   1988
Design   Paintings Margaret Shields

Artiste   AR Kane
Title   Lollita
Rec Co   4AD
Date   1987
Design   Art Dir & Design Vaughan Oliver; Photog Juergen Teller

Artiste   Tim Berne
Title   Sanctified Dreams
Rec Co   Columbia/CBS
Date   1987
Design   & Cover Art Steve Byram

Artiste   Siouxsie & The Banshees
Title   The Killing Jar
Rec Co   Polydor
Date   1988
Design   Sleeve Banshees/Nigel Vichi; Portrait Photog Alistair Thain;
           Butterflies Image Bank

Artiste   Penguin Cafe Orchestra
Title   Dirt
Rec CO   EG Records
Date   1987
Design   Bill Smith Studio

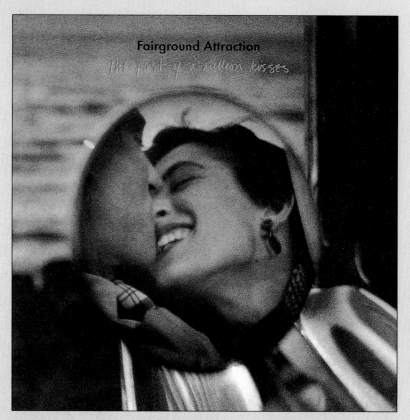

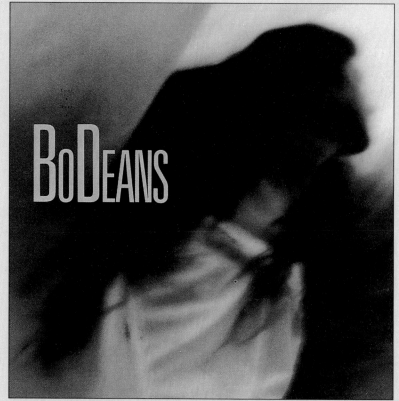

Artiste	Fairground Attraction
Title	The First of a Million Kisses
Rec Co	BMG/RCA
Date	1988
Design	Laurence Stevens; Photog Elliot Erwitt

Artiste	Main Ingredient
Title	Do Me Right
Rec Co	Chrysalis
Date	1986
Design	John Pasche; Photog Trevor Key

Artiste	Bodeans
Title	Love & Hope Sex & Dreams
Rec Co	Slash/Warner
Date	1986
Design	Art Dir Jeri McManus-Heiden; Design Jeri McManus-Heiden/ Steve J. Gerdes; Photog Matt Mahurin

Artiste	Hue & Cry
Title	I refuse
Rec Co	Circa Records
Date	1988
Design	Michael Nash Assoc; Photog Clive Warwick

diesel park west

Shakespeare Alabama

Artiste   Diesel Park West
Title   Shakespeare Alabama
Rec Co   Food/EMI
Date   1989
Design   & Art Stylorouge; Photog Simon Fowler

Artiste   Happy Mondays
Title   Bummed
Rec Co   Factory
Date   1988
Design   Central Station Design

Artiste   Little Feat
Title   Let It Roll
Rec Co   Warner
Date   1988
Design   Art Dir Janet Levinson/Neon Park; Photog Neon Park

Artiste   Antonio Carlos Jobim & The New Band
Title   Passarim
Rec Co   Verve/Polygram
Date   1987
Design   Elianne Canetti Jobim; Cover Painting Elizabeth Jobim;
           Photog Ana Lontra Jobim

Artiste   Honolulu Mountain Daffodils
Title   Tequila Dementia
Rec Co   Zinger Records
Date   1988
Design   Illus Ian Wright; Flat Visual Broadcasting

Artiste	Gaye Bykers on Acid
Title	Git Down (Shake Your Thang)
Rec Co	Virgin
Date	1987
Design	Ray Lowry

Artiste	Boy George
Title	Sold
Rec Co	Virgin
Date	1987
Design	Assorted Images

Artiste	Shakespears Sister
Title	Break My Heart/Heroine
Rec Co	London
Date	1988
Design	Laurence Stevens

Artiste	Hue & Cry
Title	Remote
Rec Co	Circa
Date	1988
Design	Michael Nash Assoc; Photog Joseph Hunwick

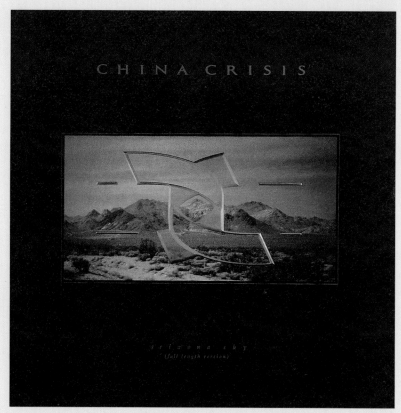

Artiste	a-ha
Title	Scoundrel Days
Rec Co	Warner
Date	1986
Design	Art Dir Jeri McManus-Heiden; Designer Jeri McManus-Heiden/ Kim Champagne; Photog Knut Bry

Artiste	Wayne Shorter
Title	Phantom Navigator
Rec Co	Imua Music
Date	1987
Design	Art Dir Tony Lane/Nancy Donald Design; Illus Jean-Francois Povedin; Sleeve Illus Wayne Shorter

Artiste	China Crisis
Title	Arizona Sky
Rec Co	Virgin
Date	1986
Design	& Photog Icon

Artiste	Chris Spheeris
Title	Pathways to Surrender
Rec Co	CBS
Date	1988
Design	Christopher Austopchuk

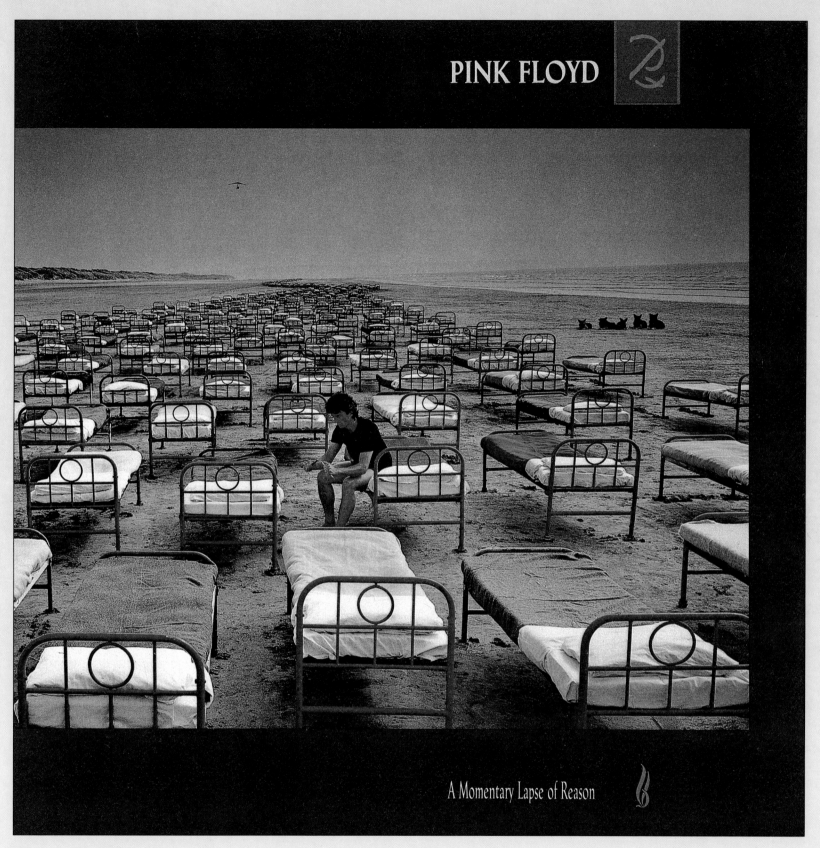

Artiste   Pink Floyd
Title   A Momentary Lapse of Reason
Rec Co   Pink Floyd Music/EMI
Date   1987
Design   Art Dir Storm Thorgerson; Front Cover Concept Storm Thorgerson/
           Nexus; Graphic Design Andrew Ellis, Icon

Artiste   Bar-Kays
Title   Animal
Rec Co   Polygram
Date   1989
Design   & Art Dir Michael Bays & Chris Thompson

Artiste   Faction
Title   Bag
Rec Co   Third Mind Records
Date   1988
Design   Titles by Faction; Design Dave Coppenhall

Artiste   Vermorel
Title   Stereo/Porno
Rec Co   Factory
Date   1988
Design   Peter Saville

Artiste   New Order
Title   Brotherhood
Rec Co   Factory
Date   1986
Design   Peter Saville Assoc; Photog Trevor Key

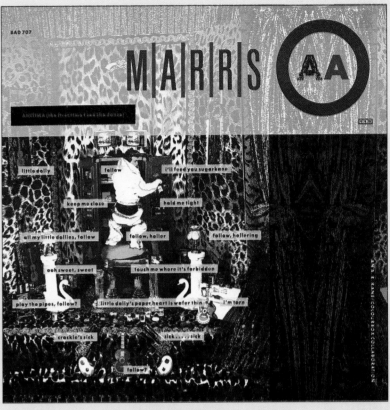

Artiste   Itchy Fingers
Title   Teranga
Rec Co   Venture/Virgin
Date   1988
Design   Icon Art Dir Richard Evans/Andrew W. Ellis

Artiste   Ultra Vivid Scene
Title   She Screamed
Rec Co   4AD
Date   1989
Design   Vaughan Oliver/v23

Artiste   M.A.R.R.S.
Title   Pump up the Volume/First Time I See She Dance
Rec Co   4AD
Design   & Art Direction Vaughan Oliver; Photog Panni Charrington

Artiste   Ornette Coleman & Prime Time
Title   Virgin Beauty
Rec Co   Portrait/CBS
Date   1988
Design   Art Dir Christopher Austopchuk

Artiste	Guns n' Roses
Title	Appetite for Destruction
Rec Co	Geffen
Date	1987
Design	Front Cover Painting Robert Williams; Art Dir & Design Michael Hodgson

Artiste	Ruinas Circulares
Title	Alpha
Rec Co	Faunus
Date	1987
Design	Osvaldo H. Vasconcelos F

Artiste	The Flesh Volcano
Title	Slut
Rec Co	Some Bizzare
Date	1987
Design	Sleeve Art Robert Williams; Layout Assorted Images

Artiste	Iron Maiden
Title	The Clairvoyant
Rec Co	BBC/EMI
Date	1988
Design	The Complete Works; Sleeve Illus Derek Riggs; Photog Ross Halfin

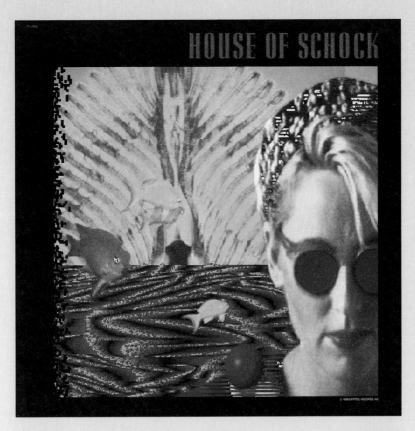

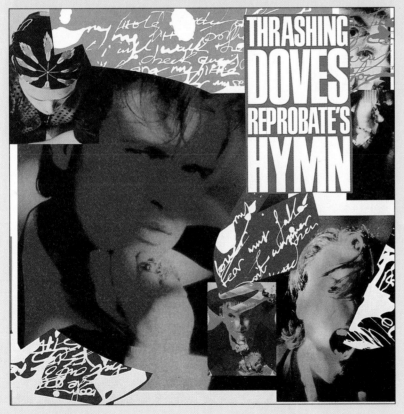

Artiste	House of Schock		Artiste	Boy George
Title	House of Schock		Title	No Clause 28
Rec Co	Capitol		Rec Co	Virgin
Date	1988		Date	1988
Design	Mike Doud		Design	Sleeve produced Jamie Reed for Assorted Images Noddy Notion Joe Ewart
Artiste	Thrashing Doves		Artiste	Madhouse
Title	Reprobates Hymn		Title	8
Rec Co	A & M		Rec Co	Paisley Park
Date	1988		Date	1987
Design	& Art Dir John Warwicker/Vivid I.D. & Jeremy Pearce		Design	& Art Dir Laura LiPuma; Photog Richard Litt

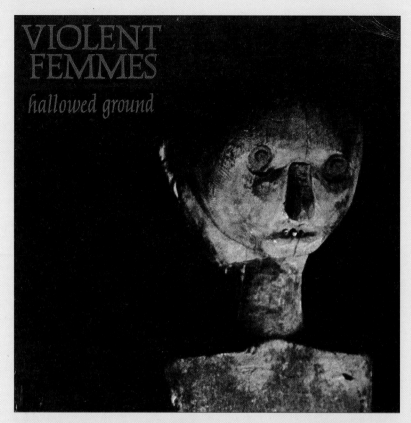

Artiste	Violent Femmes
Title	Hallowed Ground
Rec Co	Slash/Warner
Date	1984
Design	Cover Fig courtesy Larry Whitely Gallery; Art Dir Jett Price; Photog Mark Trilling

Artiste	Seigen Ono
Title	The Green Chinese Table
Rec Co	Venture/Virgin
Date	1988
Design	Sleeve Icon; Photog Michael Banks; Artwork Mekon

Artiste	David Sylvian & Holger Czukay
Title	Plight & Premonition
Rec Co	Virgin
Date	1988
Design	& Photog Yuka Fujii asstd by Icon; Artwork Mekon

Artiste	Cocteau Twins
Title	The Pink Opaque
Rec Co	4AD
Date	1985
Design	Vaughan Oliver/23 envelope; Photog Nigel Grierson/23 envelope

Every time I see you

Artiste   Fra Lippo Lippi
Title   Every Time I See You
Rec Co   Virgin
Date   1986
Design   Photog Paul Cox; Roses Johan Vipper; Design Style for Every Mood

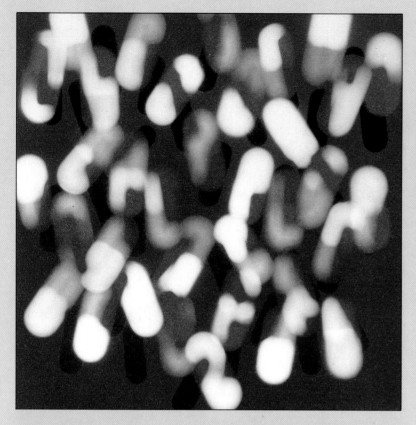

Artiste   New Order
Title   Fine Time (Remix)
Rec Co   Factory
Date   1988
Design   Cover Peter Saville Assoc; & Trevor Key after painting by
           Richard Bernstein

Artiste   Yello
Title   The Race
Rec Co   Phonogram/Mercury
Date   1988
Design   Me Company

Artiste   Wilton Felder
Title   Love is a Rush
Rec Co   MCA
Date   1987
Design   Art Dir Jeff Adamoff; Design Dir Jeff Lancaster for L-Shape Ltd;
           Illus Jeff Lancaster/Dick Bouchard; Photog Wynn Miller

Artiste   Pink Floyd
Title   One Slip
Rec Co   Pink Floyd Music/EMI
Date   1988
Design   Storm Thorgerson/Nexus; Cover Photog George Silk/Time Life

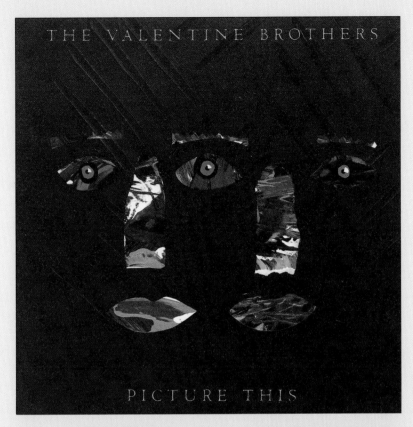

Artiste	The Valentine Brothers
Title	Picture This
Rec Co	Energy
Date	–
Design	–

Artiste	The Blow Monkeys
Title	Whoops! There Goes the Neighbourhood
Rec Co	BMG/RCA
Date	1989
Design	Michael Nash Assoc; Photog Alistair Thain

Artiste	Gentlemen without Weapons
Title	Transmissions
Rec Co	A & M
Date	1988
Design	Sleeve Storm Thorgerson/Nexus; Photog Tony May; Prod; Lance Williams; Illus Hugh Dunford Wood/Ian Wright/Jon Crossland

Artiste	Tangerine Dream
Title	Atem
Rec Co	Relativity
Date	1987
Design	Painting Edgar Froese

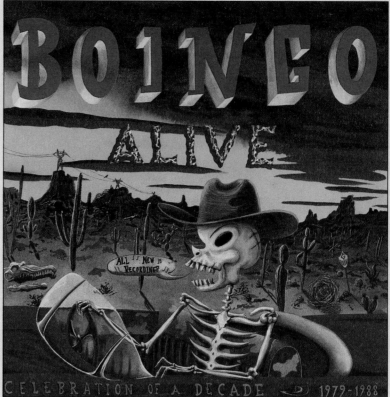

Artiste   Various compiled by David Byrne
Title   Brazil Classics — Beleza Tropical
Rec Co   Fly/EMI
Date   1989
Design   Photog Chris Callis; Design M & Co

Artiste   Louis Armstrong
Title   Stardust
Rec Co   Portrait/CBS
Date   1988
Design   Illus Patricia Dryden; Art Dir Christopher Austopchuk

Artiste   Oingo Boingo Alive
Title   Celebration of a Decade (1979-1988)
Rec Co   MCA
Date   1988
Design   Geogeanne Deen

Artiste   Living Colour
Title   Vivid
Rec Co   Epic/CBS
Date   1988
Design   Art Dir Steve Byram; Cover Art The Thunderjockeys

Artiste   Martini Ranch
Title   Holy Cow
Rec Co   Sire
Date   1988
Design   Laura LiPuma

Artiste	Deanie Ip
Title	A Thousand Suns
Rec Co	Black & White
Date	1986
Design	Tina Liu; Photog Sam Wong

Artiste	Tina Liu
Title	City Girl
Rec Co	Black & White
Date	1987
Design	Tina Liu

Artiste	Pieces of a Dream
Title	Makes You Wanna
Rec Co	EMI/Manhattan
Date	1988
Design	Art Dir Henry Marquez; Design Lu Ann Graffeo/Koppel & Scher
	Cover Illus Robert Smith; Photog Jeffrey Scales

Artiste	Pierce Turner
Title	Surface in Heaven
Rec Co	Beggars Banquet
Date	1986
Design	Christopher Bigg

Artiste	Skinny Puppy
Title	Vivi Sect Vi
Rec Co	Capitol
Date	1988
Design	Steven R. Gilmore; Asst by Nancy Miki & Barry Mah
	Typesetting Greg Sykes

Artiste	The Icicle Works
Title	Blind
Rec Co	Beggars Banquet
Date	1988
Design	Steve Hardstaff

Artiste	Cruel Story of Youth
Title	Cruel Story of Youth
Rec Co	Columbia/CBS
Date	1989
Design	Art Dir Christopher Austopchuk; Photog David La Chapelle

Artiste	Hugo Largo
Title	Mettle
Rec Co	Land
Date	1989
Design	Photog Adam Peacock; Art & Design Russell Mills/Dave Coppenhall

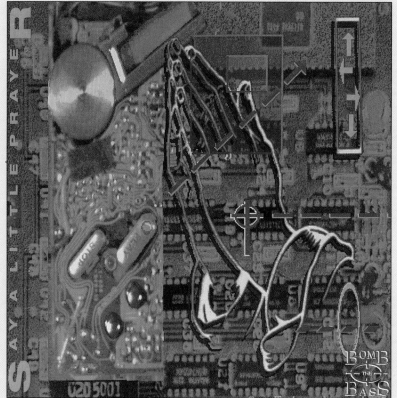

Artiste	S'Express
Title	Hey Music Lover
Rec Co	Rhythm King Records
Date	1989
Design	Pinky; Art Dir D. Little; Photog Jaco

Artiste	Living Colour
Title	Cult of Personality
Rec Co	Epic/CBS
Date	1988
Design	The Thunderjockeys for Vivid I.D.

Artiste	Bomb the Bass
Title	Say a Little Prayer
Rec Co	Rhythm King Records
Date	1988
Design	Ian Mac; Computer Images David Little/Alex Quero

Artiste	Chicago
Title	Look Away (Remix)
Rec Co	WEA
Date	1988
Design	Computer Illus Jim Hillin for deGraf/Wahrman Inc.

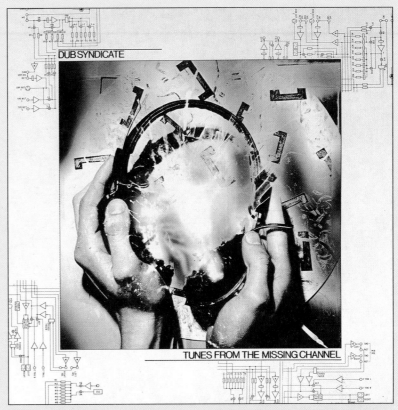

Artiste	Timex Social Club
Title	Vicious Rumours
Rec Co	Chrysalis
Date	1986
Design	Chrysalis Art; Photog Mike Prior; Illus Chris Brown

Artiste	The Comsat Angels
Title	The Cutting Edge
Rec Co	Island
Date	1986
Design	Sleeve Island Art; Photog Mike Owen; Design Michael Nash Assoc

Artiste	Dub Syndicate
Title	Tunes from the Missing Channel
Rec Co	On-U-Sound
Date	–
Design	Coney Jay/Kishi

Artiste	Hue & Cry
Title	Strength to Strength
Rec Co	Circa/Virgin
Date	1987
Design	Michael Nash Assoc; Photog Paul Kasmin

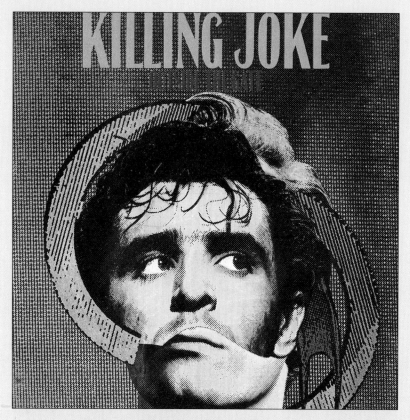

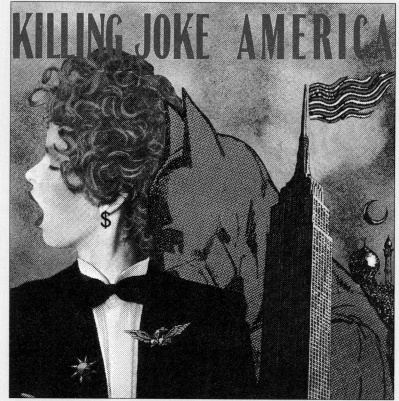

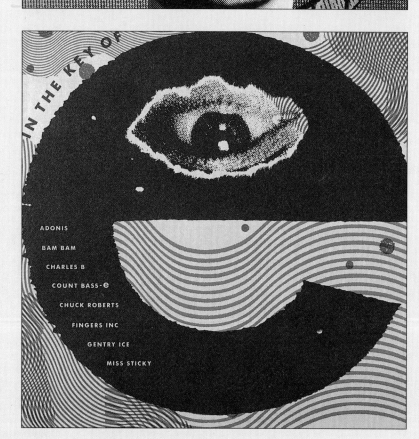

Artiste   Killing Joke
Title   Outside the Gate
Rec Co   EG/Virgin
Date   1988
Design   Bill Smith Studio; Illus Andrejz Klimowksi

Artiste   In the Key of E
Title   Luv 1
Rec Co   Desire
Date   1988
Design   Andy Vella

Artiste   Killing Joke
Title   America
Rec Co   EG/Virgin
Date   1988
Design   Bill Smith Studio; Illus Andrejz Klimowksi

Artiste   Fleetwood Mac
Title   Isn't it Midnight
Rec Co   WEA/Warner
Date   1988
Design   Jeri McManus-Heiden; Collage Ann Field

Artiste   Pink Floyd
Title   Delicate Sound of Thunder
Rec Co   CBS
Date   1988
Design   Storm Thorgerson/Colin Chambers; Photog Andy Earl/Anthony May

Artiste	Jane Ira Bloom
Title	Slalom
Rec Co	CBS
Date	1988
Design	Christopher Austopchuk; Illus Karen Caldicott; Photog Kristine Larsen

Artiste	The Dukes of Stratosphear
Title	Psonic Psunspot
Rec Co	Virgin
Date	1987
Design	Cover Art Sir John Johns The Irreverent Neon Paisley and Psychoderek

Artiste	Shame
Title	Going Down the River
Rec Co	Shake the Record Label
Date	1986
Design	Photog Norman Rodger; Graphics/Layout Ally Palmer

Artiste	Los Lobos
Title	How Will the Wolf Survive?
Rec Co	Slash/Warner
Date	1984
Design	& Art Dir Kav Deluxe; Illus Elizabeth Brady

Artiste   Beastie Boys
Title   The Beastie Boys
Rec Co   Def Jam/CBS
Date   1986
Design   —

Artiste   Talking Heads
Title   Stop Making Sense
Rec Co   Sire/Warner
Date   1984
Design   Cover Photog Adelle Lutz; Design David Byrne, Michael Hodgson,
           Jeff Ayeroff

Artiste   Richard H. Kirk
Title   Black Jesus Voice
Rec Co   Rough Trade/Island
Date   1986
Design   Naked Art; Sleeve Images Phil Barnes

Artiste   Various
Title   Acid 1
Rec Co   Hot Melt
Date   1988
Design   Sleeve Toni & Section 3

Artiste   Various
Title   North the Sound of the Dance Underground
Rec Co   De Construction Records
Date   1988
Design   Artwork Central Station Design

Artiste   Various
Title   Acido Amigo
Rec Co   Westside
Date   1988
Design   Idest

Artiste   Duranduran
Title   All she Wants is (US Master mix)
Rec Co   EMI
Date   1988
Design   Hans Arnold

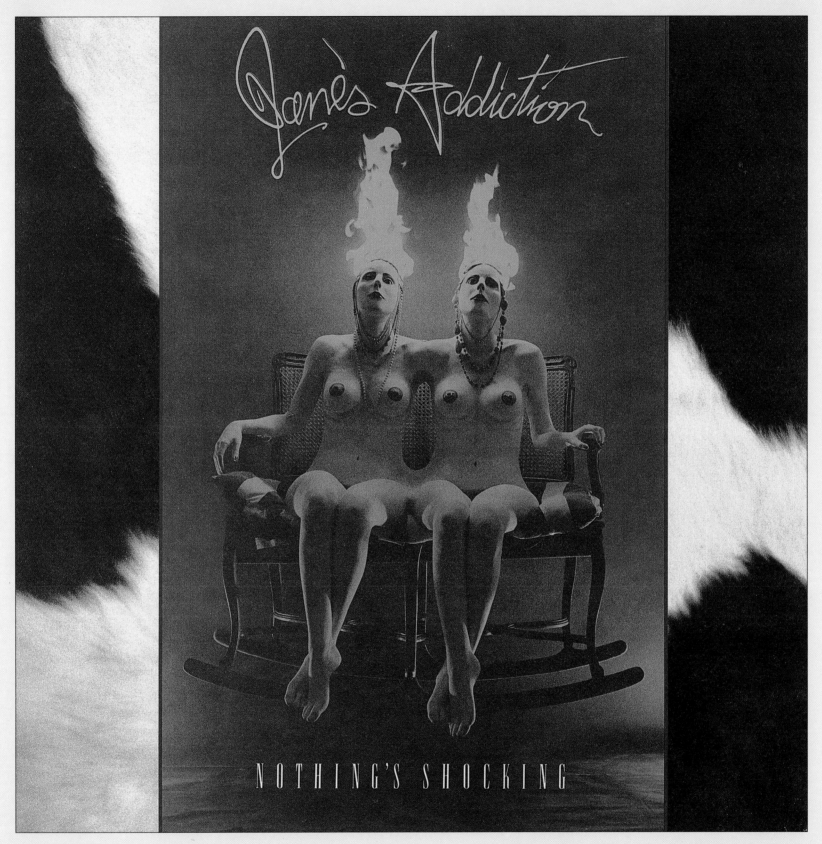

Artiste   Jane's Addiction
Title   Nothing's Shocking
Rec Co   Warner
Date   1988
Design   Photog Perry Farrell; Art Dir Kim Champagne; Sculpture Perry Farrell

Artiste	Gaye Bykers on Acid
Title	Stewed to the Gills...
Rec Co	Virgin
Date	1989
Design	& Photog Peter Anderson, Clare Cameron, Gaye Bykers on Acid

Artiste	Sumo Giants
Title	Foolish Things (12″)
Rec Co	Metro
Date	1988
Design	Cover Art RJ Nicholls of Mindscapes; Layout Anita Plank

Artiste	Stewart Copeland
Title	The Equaliser & other Cliff Hangers
Rec Co	IRS/No Speak
Date	1987
Design	& Art Dir The Leisure Process; Photog Andrew Douglas

Artiste	Tesla
Title	Mechanical Resonance
Rec Co	Geffen/Warner
Date	1986
Design	Photog Dean Chamberlain

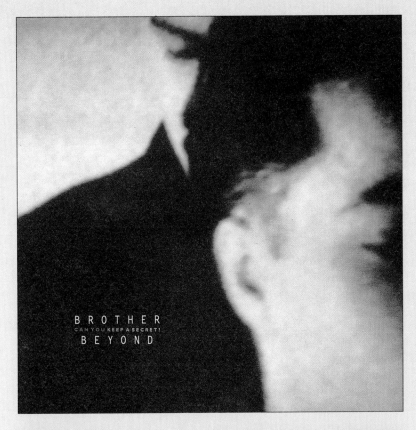

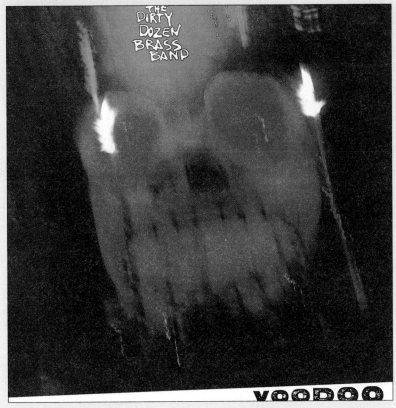

Artiste   Brother Beyond
Title   Can You Keep a Secret?
Rec Co   EMI
Date   1987
Design   Sleeve Mark Farrow at 3 & Sheila Rock

Artiste   The Dirty Dozen Brass Band
Title   Voodoo
Rec Co   Rounder/Columbia
Date   1989
Design   Art Dir Christopher Austopchuk; Photog David Katzenstein

Artiste   The Radiators (New Orleans)
Title   Law of the Fish
Rec Co   Epic/CBS
Date   1987
Design   Art Dir Christopher Austopchuk; Photog Chip Simons

Artiste   Osamu
Title   Passages
Rec Co   CBS
Date   1987
Design   Art Dir Joel Zimmerman; Photog Ron Morecraft

Artiste   Sam Hui
Title   Sam Hui
Rec Co   Cinepoly
Date   1986
Design   & Artworks The Communicator; Photog Jonny Koo Concept & Art Dir
           William Szeto

Artiste   Bill Watrous
Title   Reflections
Rec Co   Soundwings
Date   1987
Design   Jeff Lancaster for L-Shape; Illus Lou Beach

Artiste   Various
Title   Pop Inside the 60s
Rec Co   See for Miles
Date   1988
Design   Picture courtesy of Lovable; Idea Colin Miles

Artiste   Marti Jones
Title   Used Guitars
Rec Co   A & M
Date   1987
Design   Melanie Nissen; Photog Deborah Feingold/Robert Bean

Artiste   Dave Pike
Title   Pikes Peak
Rec Co   Portrait/CBS
Date   1989
Design   Art Dir Stacy Drummond; Illus Henrik Drescher; Photog Hank Parker

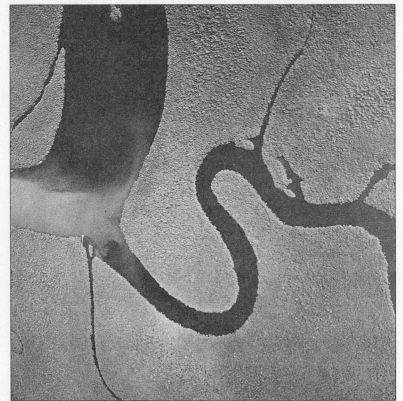

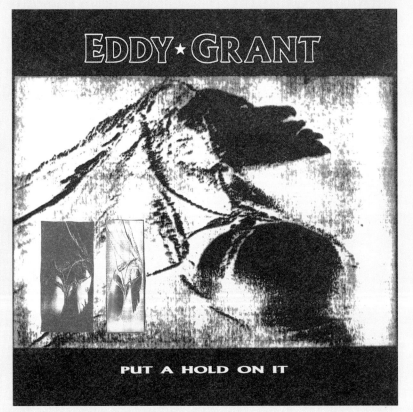

Artiste	Gentlemen without Weapons
Title	Transmissions
Rec Co	A & M
Date	1988
Design	Storm Thorgerson

Artiste	The Armoury Show
Title	Waiting for the Floods
Rec Co	EMI/Capitol
Date	1985
Design	–

Artiste	Dead Can Dance
Title	Serpents Egg
Rec Co	4AD
Date	1988
Design	Brendan Perry & Vaughan Oliver

Artiste	Eddy Grant
Title	Put a Hold on it (12″)
Rec Co	Blue Wave/EMI/Parlaphone
Date	1988
Design	Abrahams Pants; Photog Paul Cox

Artiste	Pixies
Title	Monkey Gone to Heaven
Rec Co	4AD
Date	1989
Design	& Art Dir Vaughan Oliver at v23; Photog Simon Larbalestier

Artiste	Climie Fisher
Title	Love Like a River
Rec Co	EMI
Date	1988
Design	Bill Smith Studio; Studio Photog Sara Wilson

Artiste	Horseland
Title	Love Dies Again
Rec Co	Red Rhino Records
Date	1988
Design	& Art Dir Vaughan Oliver at v23 envelope; Photog Diana Grandi

Artiste	Peter Hope & Richard H. Kirk
Title	Hoodoo Talk
Rec Co	Native Records
Date	1987
Design	Artwork & Addit Design The Designers from concept by Naked Art; Photog Philip Barnes

Artiste   Yello
Title   One Second
Rec Co   Phonogram/Mercury
Date   1987
Design   Ernst Gamper

Artiste   Spear of Destiny
Title   Never Take Me Alive
Rec Co   10/Virgin
Date   1987
Design   Stylorouge; Illus Chris Welch

Artiste   Depeche Mode
Title   Never Let me Down Again
Rec Co   Mute
Date   1987
Design   T & CP Associates

Artiste   James
Title   Yaho
Rec Co   Sire/WEA
Date   1987
Design   –

PART TWO
THE GRAPHIC APPROACH

To catch the eye of the public is obviously one of the main motives for album design. The graphic approach is a favoured device to grab attention. A geometry of shapes, or a formality of layout, are used in a host of different ways. Sometimes it is a virtual emptiness (page 60) or plain type (opposite). At other times it is severe abstraction (58), or an elegant flourish (65).

And at others still it is vibrant colour, deployed harshly as on page 77, or used in an ethnic context (75). Black and white photography, illustration, tint lays, old photos, lino cuts, you name it. If is works, use it. There's no morality in rock 'n' roll, only groove and change. Or so they tell me.

These songs were recorded *live* by **The Fountainhead** at the Whisky in Hollywood on Tuesday 9th December 1986, at the final show of the band's debut U.S. tour. **'So Good Now', 'Heart & Soul'** & **'Sometimes'** were co-produced *overnight* by Mike Frondelli and The Fountainhead.

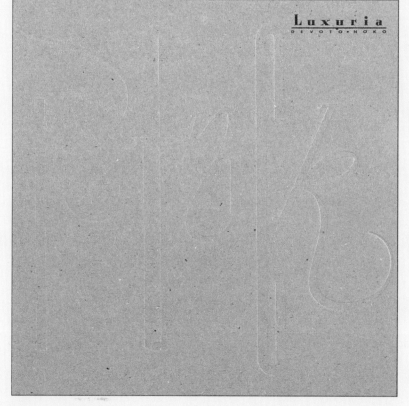

Artiste	Throwing Muses
Title	Hunkpapa
Rec Co	4AD
Date	1989
Design	–

Artiste	The Fountainhead
Title	So Good Now
Rec Co	China/Chrysalis
Date	1987
Design	Stephen Horse

Artiste	Rainy Day
Title	Rainy Day
Rec Co	Rough Trade
Date	1984
Design	Kendra Smith

Artiste	Luxuria Devoto Noko
Title	Red Neck
Rec Co	Beggars Banquet
Date	1988
Design	Christopher Bigg

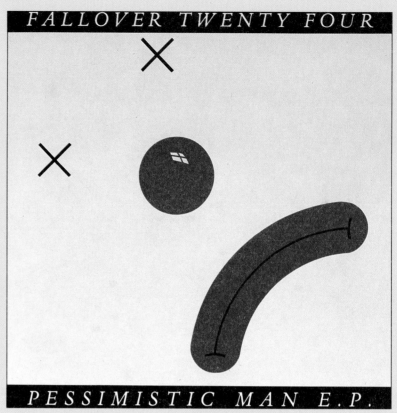

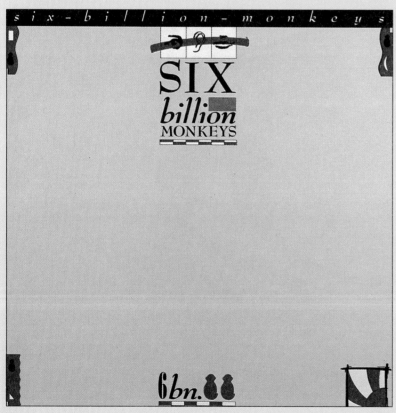

Artiste   Simple Minds
Title   Ghostdancing/Jungleland
Rec Co   Virgin
Date   1986
Design   –

Artiste   Six-billion Monkeys
Title   Six-billion Monkeys
Rec Co   Moogungwha
Date   1987
Design   & Art Over the Moon

Artiste   Fallover 24
Title   Pessimistic Man
Rec Co   Ugly Man Records
Date   1989
Design   Carl Waite

Artiste   Keith and Julie Tippett
Title   Couple in Spirit
Rec Co   EG/Virgin
Date   1988
Design   De Facto; Illus Ian Whadcock

Artiste	Leroy Carr
Title	Blues before Sunrise
Rec Co	Portrait/CBS
Date	1989
Design	Art Dir Stacy Drummond; Illus Neil Shigley

Artiste	Well Red
Title	Yes We Can
Rec Co	Virgin
Date	1987
Design	David Crow at Assorted Images

Artiste	Mick Jagger
Title	Primitive Cool
Rec Co	CBS
Date	1987
Design	Art Dir Christopher Austopchuk; Illus Francesco Clemente

Artiste	Julian Jonah
Title	Jealousy and Lies
Rec Co	Chrysalis
Date	1988
Design	John Pasche; Photog Mark Lewis

Artiste   Laugh
Title   Sensation No. 1 (12″)
Rec Co   Sub Aqua
Date   1988
Design   Luke Hayes

Artiste   Yello
Title   Tied Up
Rec Co   Phonogram
Date   1986
Design   Me Company

Artiste   The Style Council
Title   The Cost of Loving
Rec Co   Polydor
Date   1987
Design   Style Council/Simon Halfin; Photog Nick Knight

Artiste   Robert Wyatt
Title   Old Rottenhat
Rec Co   Rough Trade
Date   1985
Design   Caryn Gough/Multi-Modis; Cover Paintings Alfreda Benge

Artiste   Front Line Assembly
Title   Gashed Senses and Crossfire
Rec Co   Third Mind Records
Date   1989
Design   Sleeve artwork Dave Coppenhall

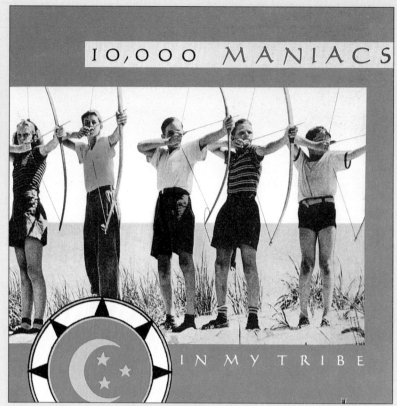

Artiste   The Big Dish
Title   Prospect Street (12")
Rec Co   Virgin
Date   1986
Design   & Art Dir Gary Wathen; Design Red Ranch & Gowans

Artiste   Take 6
Title   Doo de doo wop bop!
Rec Co   Reprise/Warner
Date   1988
Design   Kaz Deluxe

Artiste   10,000 Maniacs
Title   In My Tribe
Rec Co   Elektra/Asylum/Warner
Date   1987
Design   Kosh

Artiste   Ultra Vivid Scene
Title   Ultra Vivid Scene
Rec Co   4AD
Date   1988
Design   Vaughan Oliver/v23

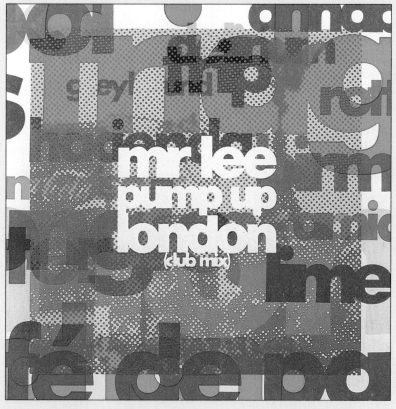

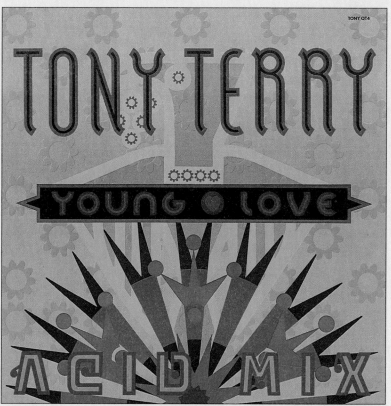

Artiste   World Domination Enterprises
Title   Lets Play Domination
Rec Co   Product Inc
Date   1988
Design   World Domination Enterprises & Slim Smith; Photog Lawrence Watson

Artiste   Mr Lee
Title   Pump up London (12″)
Rec Co   A & M
Date   1988
Design   Graham (i-design) Tunna

Artiste   Various
Title   House Hallucinates Pump up London volume 1
Rec Co   A & M
Date   1988
Design   Sleeve Graham (I don't dance) Tunna with aid from Jeremy Pearce

Artiste   Tony Terry
Title   Young Love (12″)
Rec Co   Epic/CBS
Date   1988
Design   Sleeve design pruned at Mainartery

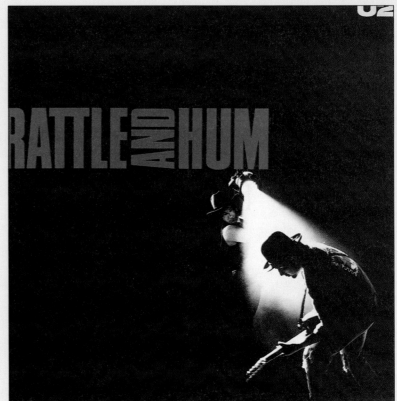

Artiste   Xmal Deutschland
Title   Sickle Moon
Rec Co   Phonogram
Date   1987
Design   Vaughan Oliver; Photog Wolfgang Ellerbrock

Artiste   Frazier Chorus
Title   Dream Kitchen
Rec Co   Virgin
Date   1988
Design   Bill Smith Studio & Frazier Chorus; Photog The Douglas Brothers

Artiste   U2
Title   Rattle and Hum
Rec Co   Island
Date   1988
Design   Steve DZN; Photog Anton Corbin

Artiste   Luxuria Devoto Noko
Title   Unanswerable Lust
Rec Co   Beggars Banquet
Date   1988
Design   Christopher Bigg

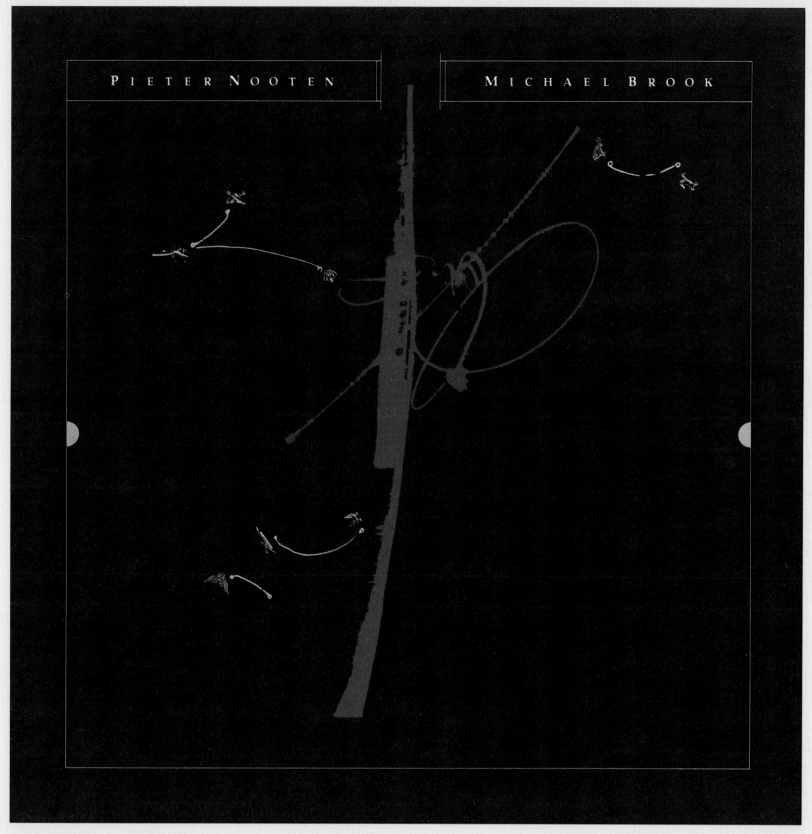

Artiste   Peter Nooten, Michael Brook
Title   Sleeps with the Fishes
Rec Co   4AD
Date   1987
Design   Art Dir & Design Vaughan Oliver; Calligraphy Christopher Bigg

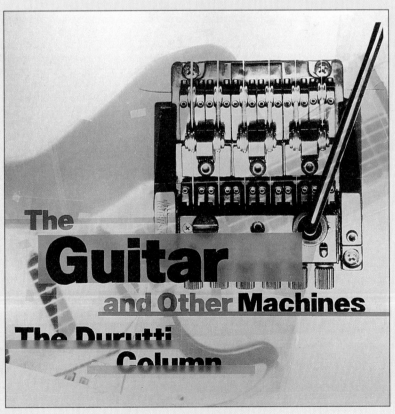

Artiste   UB40
Title   UB40
Rec Co   A & M/Virgin
Date   1988
Design   Shoot That Tiger!; Paintings Steve Masterson

Artiste   The Durutti Column
Title   The Guitar and other Machines
Rec Co   Factory
Date   1988
Design   Mark Holt/8vo; Photog Trevor Key

Artiste   Ivan Nevill
Title   If my Ancestors could see me Now
Rec Co   Polygram/Polydor
Date   1988
Design   Larry Vigan Studio

Artiste   Simple Minds
Title   I Travel
Rec Co   Virgin
Date   1979
Design   Sleeve Assorted Images; Photog Garry Mouat

the

d u R u TT i

C o l u m n .

WITHOUT MERCY

fac 84

Artiste   The Durutti Column
Title   Without Mercy
Rec Co   Factory
Date   1989
Design   Typographic Design 8vo

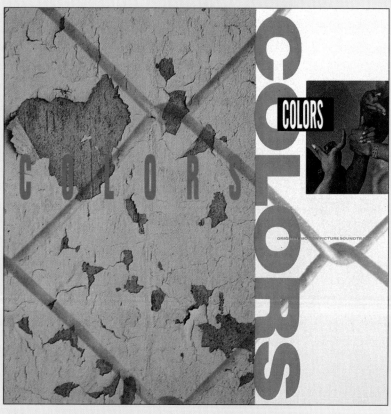

Artiste   Arthur Blythe
Title   Basic Blythe
Rec Co   Columbia/CBS
Date   1988
Design   Art Dir Stacy Drummond; Cover Illus Peter Kuper;
             Photog Nancy LeLine

Artiste   –
Title   Colors-original motion picture soundtrack
Rec Co   Warner
Date   1988
Design   Art Dir Deborah Norcross/Jeri MacManus-Heiden
             Photog David Skernick/Merrick Morton

Artiste   Cruzados
Title   After Dark
Rec Co   Arista
Date   1987
Design   Maude Silman

Artiste   Scratch Acid
Title   Scratch Acid
Rec Co   Fundamental
Date   1986
Design   Mark Todd

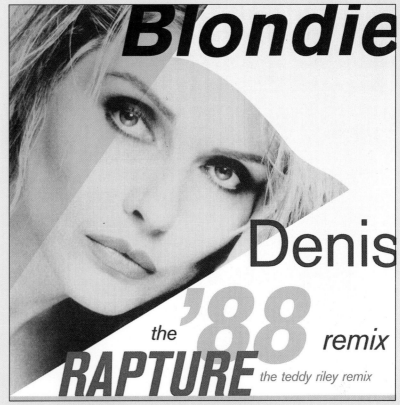

Artiste   The Fall
Title   The Frenz Experiment
Rec Co   Beggars Banquet/Warner
Date   1988
Design   Photog Paul Cox

Artiste   Thrashing Doves
Title   Angel Visit
Rec Co   A & M
Date   1989
Design   & Art Dir John Warwicker/Vivid I.D. and Jeremy Pearce;
          Photog Enrique Badulescu

Artiste   Blondie
Title   Denis (88 remix)
Rec Co   Chrysalis
Date   1988
Design   John Pasche; Photog Brian Aris

Artiste   Thrashing Doves
Title   Trouble in the Home
Rec Co   A & M
Date   1989
Design   & Art Dir John Warwicker/Vivid I.D. and Jeremy Pearce;
          Photog Enrique Badulescu

Artiste	Yello
Title	Desire (12″)
Rec Co	WEA/Warner
Date	1985
Design	Ernst Gamper

Artiste	Curiosity Killed the Cat
Title	Free
Rec Co	Phonogram
Date	1987
Design	The Unknown

Artiste	Timbuk 3
Title	Eden Alley
Rec Co	International Record Syndicate/Warner
Date	1988
Design	& Art Dir Carlos Grasso & Ron Scarselli

Artiste	Various
Title	Music for Films
Rec Co	Land
Date	1988
Design	Russell Mills; Cover Drawing Brian Eno; Photog Jeff Veitch

Artiste   Duke Ellington
Title   The Blanton-Webster Band
Rec Co   Bluebird/RCA
Date   1988
Design   —

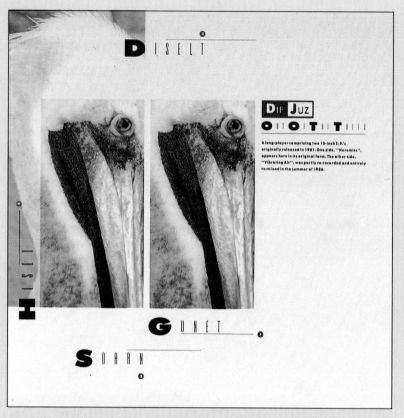

Artiste   Dif Juz
Title   Out of the Trees
Rec Co   4AD
Date   1986
Design   Vaughan Oliver/23 envelope; Photog Nigel Grierson/23 envelope

Artiste   Janet Jackson
Title   Control
Rec Co   A & M
Date   1986
Design   Art Dir Chuck Beeson/Melanie Nissen; Photog Tony Viramontes

Artiste   Makoto Ozone
Title   Now You Know
Rec Co   CBS
Date   1988
Design   Allen Wemberg

Artiste   Horse
Title   You Could be Forgiven (12″)
Rec Co   Capitol/EMI
Date   1989
Design   Artwork The Artful Dodgers Ltd

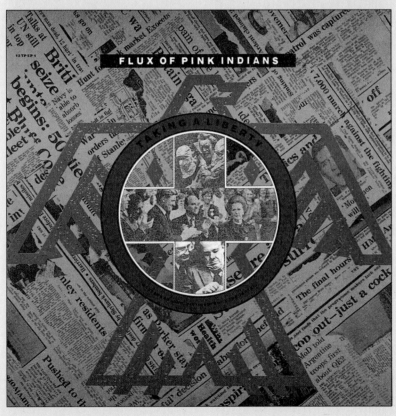

Artiste	The Fall
Title	Victoria (12″)
Rec Co	Beggars Banquet
Date	1988
Design	Photog Arabella Ashley

Artiste	Flux of Pink Indians
Title	Taking a Liberty
Rec Co	One Little Indian Records
Date	—
Design	Photog Derek Birkett; Design & Illus Me Company

Artiste	U.T.F.O.
Title	We Work Hard
Rec Co	Cool Tempo/Chrysalis
Date	1986
Design	Stephen Horse

Artiste	Glen Burtnick
Title	Heard it on the Radio (12″)
Rec Co	A & M
Date	1987
Design	Sarah Southin; Photog Jim Rakete

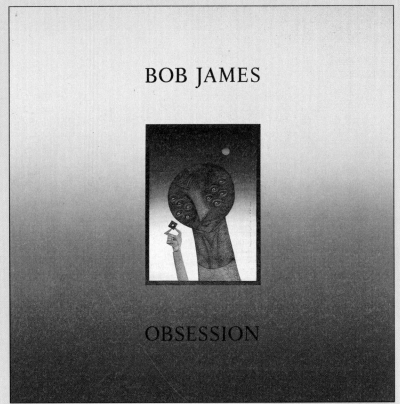

Artiste   New Order
Title   Technique
Rec Co   Factory
Date   1989
Design   Peter Saville Assoc; and Trevor Key

Artiste   What If
Title   What If
Rec Co   RCA
Date   1987
Design   Norman Moore

Artiste   Bob James
Title   Obsession
Rec Co   Warner
Date   1986
Design   Art Dir Laura LiPuma; Illus Eric Blum

Artiste   Sally Timmy & The Drifting Cowgirls
Title   Somebody's Rocking my Dreamboat
Rec Co   Tim/Red Rhino/Cartel
Date   1988
Design   Painting Emma Boland; Artwork 13 Limns

Artiste   Orchestral Manoeuvres in the Dark
Title   The Pacific Age
Rec Co   Virgin
Date   1986
Design   Package Art Mick Haggerty

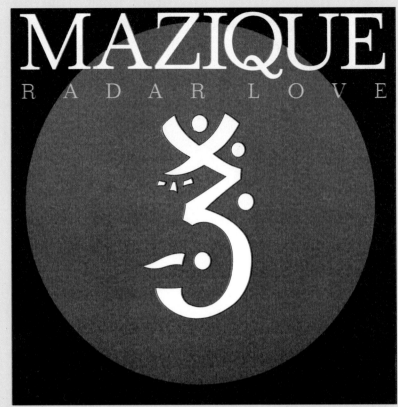

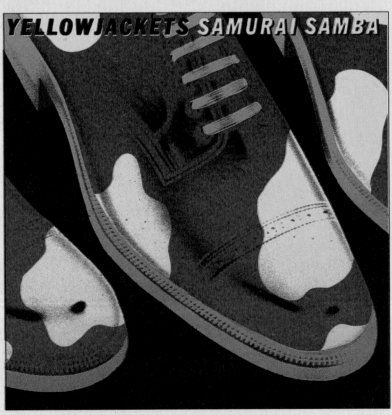

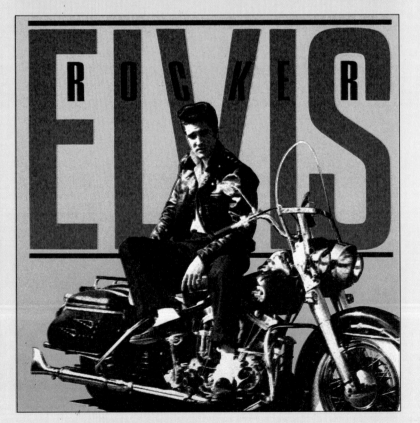

Artiste   Steve Miller Band
Title   Greatest Hits 1976-1986
Rec Co   Sailor/Phonogram
Date   1987
Design   Tommy Steele; Art Dir Steve Miller

Artiste   Yellowjackets
Title   Samurai Samba
Rec Co   Warner
Date   1985
Design   & Art Dir Simon Levy; Cover Artwork Lou Beach; Photog Jeff Katz

Artiste   Mazique
Title   Radar Love
Rec Co   Rage
Date   1988
Design   Guy Stanway

Artiste   Elvis Presley
Title   Rocker
Rec Co   RCA
Date   1984
Design   Cover Courtesy Harley-Davidson Motor Co; Art Dir Ron Kellum

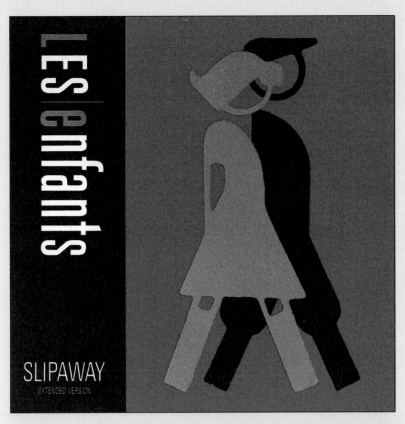

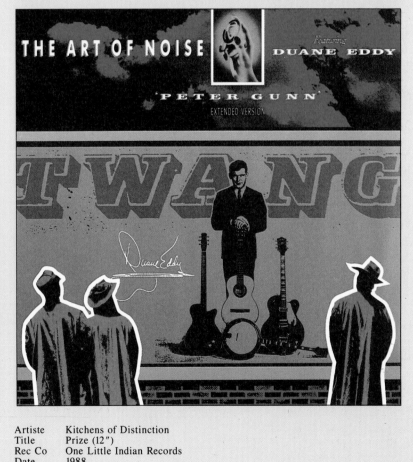

Artiste   Les Enfants
Title   Slipaway
Rec Co   Chrysalis
Date   1985
Design   John Pasche

Artiste   Various
Title   One Little Indian take on the cowboys with Greatest Hits Vol. 1
Rec Co   One Little Indian Records
Date   1988
Design   Me Company

Artiste   Kitchens of Distinction
Title   Prize (12″)
Rec Co   One Little Indian Records
Date   1988
Design   Me Company

Artiste   The Art of Noise featuring Duane Eddy
Title   "Peter Gunn"
Rec Co   China/Chrysalis
Date   1986
Design   John Pasche

Artiste   John Lennon
Title   Imagine — John Lennon. Music from the motion picture
Rec Co   EMI
Date   1988
Design   John Pasche

Artiste   Deacon Blue
Title   Real Gone Kid
Rec Co   CBS
Date   1988
Design   Bridges & Woods

Artiste   The Art of Noise
Title   Legs
Rec Co   China/Chrysalis
Date   1985
Design   John Pasche

Artiste   Habit
Title   Medicine Man
Rec Co   Virgin
Date   1988
Design   Mark Farrow/Three Assoc; Photog Sheila Rock

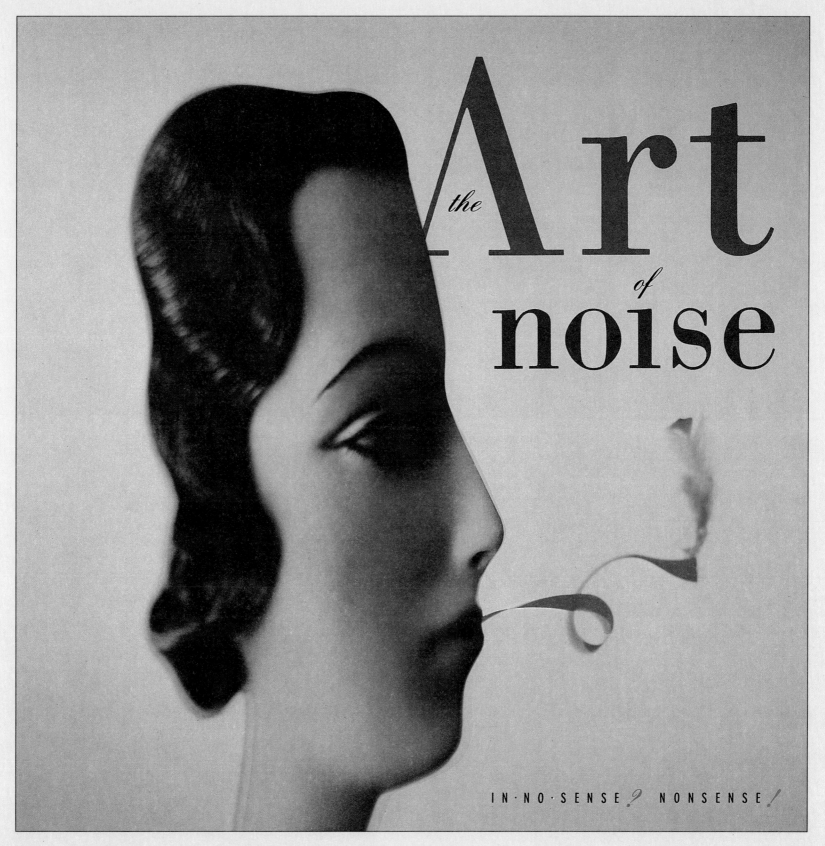

Artiste   The Art of Noise
Title   In no Sense? Nonsense!
Rec Co   China/Chrysalis
Date   1987
Design   Design typographics Roland Williams; Photog Alan David-Tu
           Art Dir John Pasche

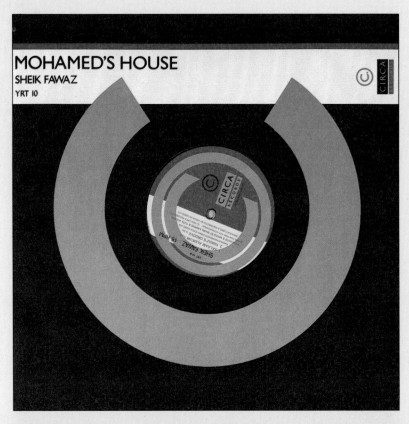

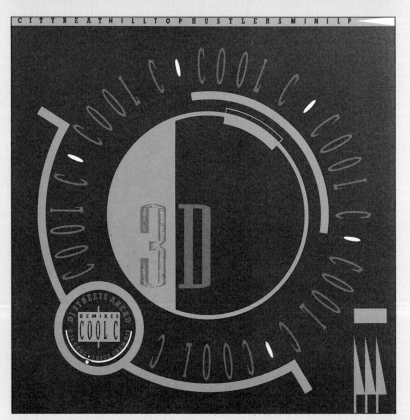

Artiste   Sheik Fawaz
Title   Mohamed's House
Rec Co   Circa/Virgin
Date   1988
Design   Michael Nash Assoc

Artiste   M.A.R.R.S.
Title   Pump up the Volume (Remix)
Rec Co   4AD
Date   1987
Design   & Art Dir Vaughan Oliver; Photog Panni Charrington

Artiste   Roxanne Shante
Title   Go On Girl
Rec Co   A & M
Date   1988
Design   Graham Tunna

Artiste   Cool C & 3D
Title   Hilltop Hustlers
Rec Co   City Beat
Date   1988
Design   Christopher Bigg

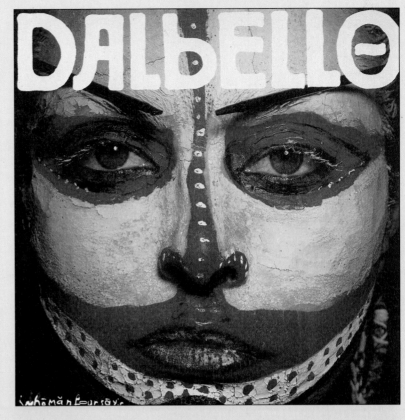

Artiste   Duranduran
Title   Big Thing
Rec Co   EMI
Date   1988
Design   Hans Arnold; Photog Virginia Liberatore

Artiste   The Crusaders
Title   Life in the Modern World
Rec Co   MCA
Date   1988
Design   Jeff Lancaster for L-Shape; Art Dir Jeff Adamoff;
            Illus Leif Olson

Artiste   Dalbello
Title   Whomanfoursays
Rec Co   Capitol/EMI
Date   1984
Design   & Art Dir Heather Brown; Hand Lettering Mary Margaret O'Hara;
            Photog Deborah Samuel

Artiste   Renegade Sound Wave
Title   Biting my nails (12″)
Rec Co   Mute
Date   1988
Design   David Little

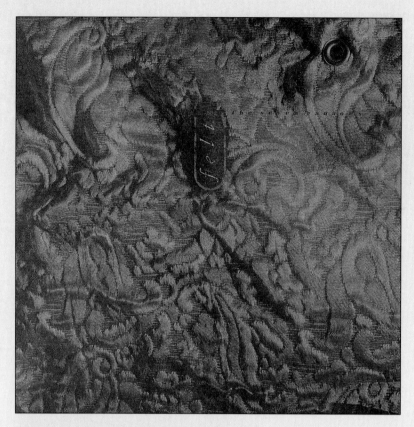

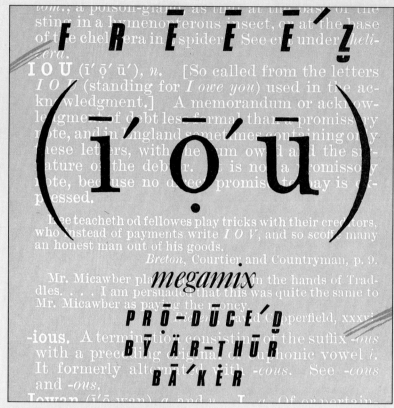

Artiste Felt
Title Ignite the Seven Canons
Rec Co Cherry Red
Date 1985
Design Ross & Bigg

Artiste Climie Fisher
Title Love Changes (Everything)
Rec Co EMI
Date 1987
Design Bill Smith Studio; Photog Carrie Branoran

Artiste Freeez
Title I.O.U.
Rec Co Beggars Banquet
Date 1983
Design The London Design Partnership; Designer Gerry O'Dwyer

Artiste Le Mystere des voix Bulgares
Title Le Mystere des voix Bulgares (vol 1)
Rec Co 4AD
Date 1986
Design Vaughan Oliver/23 envelope; Photog Nigel Grierson/23 envelope

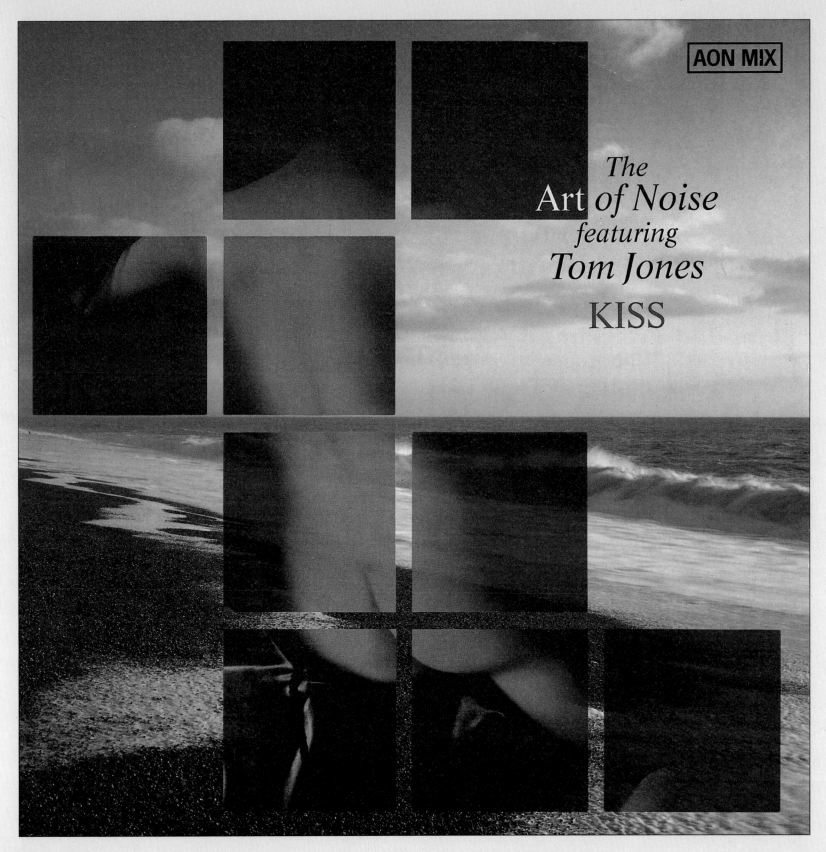

AON MIX

The
Art *of Noise*
featuring
Tom Jones

KISS

Artiste   The Art of Noise — featuring Tom Jones
Title   Kiss
Rec Co   China/Polydor
Date   1988
Design   Ryan Art; Photog Paul Wakefield/Anna Hodgson

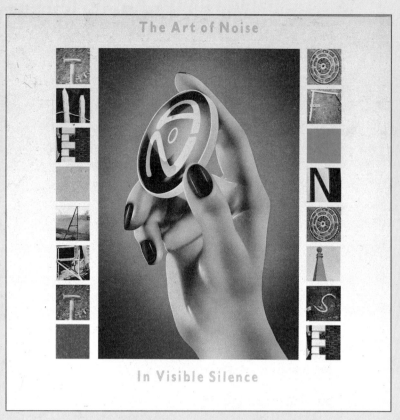

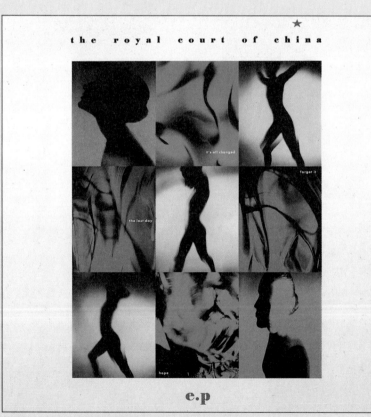

Artiste	The Art of Noise
Title	In Visible Silence
Rec Co	China/Chrysalis
Date	1986
Design	John Pasche

Artiste	The Royal Court of China
Title	The Royal Court of China
Rec Co	A & M
Date	1987
Design	Jeremy Pearce; Photog Andy Bettles

Artiste	The Smithereens
Title	Green Thoughts
Rec Co	Enigma/Capitol
Date	1988
Design	Tommy Steele/Jeff Lancaster for L-Shape; Art Dir Tommy Steele/ Pat DiNizio

Artiste	Christopher Wong
Title	Christopher
Rec Co	Philips/Polygram
Date	1988
Design	Stan Chung; Photog Leung Kar Tai

PART THREE
PORTRAITS

'Sell the image, sell the record − put the artiste's face on the cover' − these are maxims of the record company's marketing department. True in 1963; true today? It is often the designer's nightmare − asked to put the boat race on the front AND make the design really interesting. This is so difficult to do since there have been more portraits on album packaging than anything else. How to ring the changes?

ACA 5 is therefore proud to present some of the really great changes that have been rung, in particular the painting/photo mix of Enya (page 93) and the textural Kitaro (97), the humour of Prince (101), the cleverness of Sade (100) and the sinister mood of Bryan Ferry (88,94). Even if you didn't ask, I think, personally, that these are the best portraits seen in a long time.

Artiste	Terence Trent D'Arby
Title	Introducing the Hardline according to Terence Trent D'Arby
Rec Co	CBS
Date	1987
Design	Peter Barrett asstd by Andrew Biscomb

Artiste	Branford Marsalis
Title	Renaissance
Rec Co	Columbia/CBS
Date	1987
Design	Photog Roy DeCarava; Art Dir Arnold Levine

Artiste	Peter Murphy
Title	Tale of the Tongue
Rec Co	Beggars Banquet
Date	1986
Design	Denise Richardson; Photog Jim Costello

Artiste	Hue & Cry
Title	Seduced and Abandoned
Rec Co	Circa
Date	1987
Design	Michael Nash Assoc; Photog Jean-Baptiste Mondino

PATTI
SMITH

DREAM
OF
LIFE

LLOYD COLE AND THE COMMOTIONS . MY BAG

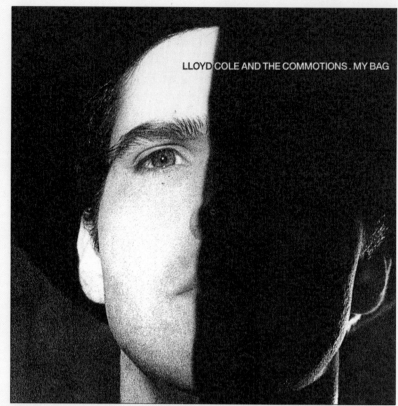

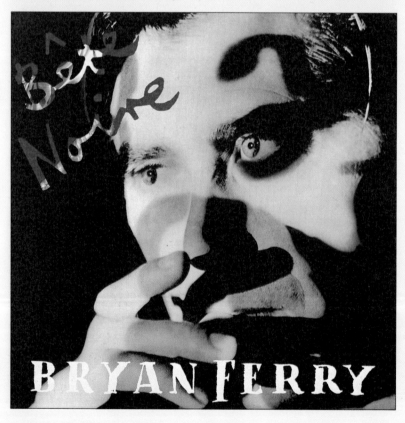

BRYAN FERRY

NIK KERSHAW

ONE STEP AHEAD

INDUSTRIAL MIX

Artiste	Patti Smith
Title	Dream of Life
Rec Co	Arista
Date	1988
Design	Photog Robert Mapplethorpe

Artiste	Bryan Ferry
Title	Bete Noir
Rec Co	Reprise/Warner
Date	1987
Design	Bryan Ferry/Andrew Reid

Artiste	Lloyd Cole & The Commotions
Title	My Bag (12″)
Rec Co	Polydor
Date	1987
Design	Michael Nash Assoc; Photog Alistair Thain

Artiste	Nik Kershaw
Title	One Step Ahead
Rec Co	MCA
Date	1988
Design	& Art Dir Stylorouge; Photog Nic Georghiou

BLACK

EVERYTHING'S

COMING UP

ROSES

Artiste   Black
Title   Everything's Coming Up Roses
Rec Co   A & M
Date   1987
Design   & Art Dir John Warwicker; Photog Nigel Grierson/23 envelope

Artiste   Marshall Crenshaw
Title   Mary Jean & 9 others
Rec Co   Warner
Date   1987
Design   Art Dir Nick Egan; Photog Dean Chamberlain

Artiste   Good Question
Title   Good Question
Rec Co   Paisley Park
Date   1988
Design   Art Dir Laura LiPuma; Photog Taylor King

Artiste   Bros
Title   I owe you nothing (12″)
Rec Co   CBS
Date   1988
Design   Three Assoc; Photog Chris Nash

Artiste   Sammy Hagar
Title   Sammy Hagar
Rec Co   Geffen
Date   1987
Design   Gabrielle Raumberger

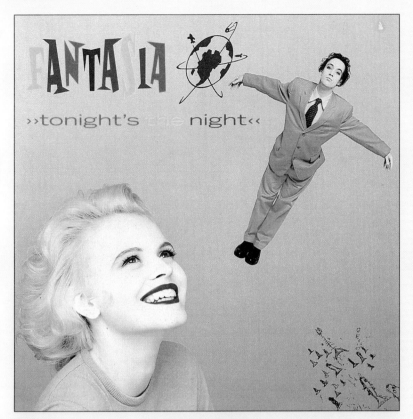

Artiste	Fantasia
Title	Tonights the Night
Rec Co	Chrysalis
Date	1988
Design	John Warwicker

Artiste	Voice of the Beehive
Title	Let it Bee
Rec Co	London
Date	1988
Design	& Art Dir Vivid I.D. Photog Mike Owen Illus Jerry Lee

Artiste	Voice of the Beehive
Title	Don't Call Me Baby
Rec Co	London
Date	1988
Design	& Art Dir Vivid I.D.; Photog Mike Owen

Artiste	The Go-Betweens
Title	16 Lovers Lane
Rec Co	Beggars Banquet
Date	1988
Design	John Willsteed; Photog Robyn Stacey; Hand Lettering Amanda Brown

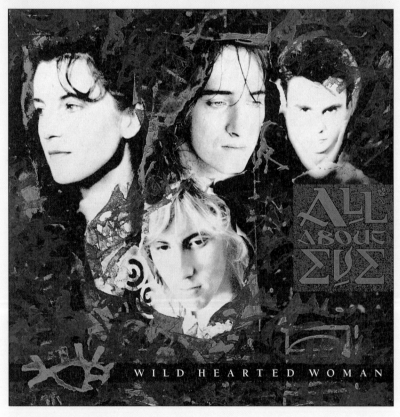

Artiste   Siouxsie & The Banshees
Title   Peep Show
Rec Co   Polydor
Date   1988
Design   C. More Tone Studios; Photog Alistair Thain

Artiste   All About Eve
Title   Wild Hearted Woman
Rec Co   Phonogram
Date   1988
Design   & Art Dir Stylorouge; Photog Tansy Spinks; Photog Treatment
            Anne Nicol

Artiste   Skinny Puppy
Title   Cleanse Fold & Manipulate
Rec Co   Capitol
Date   1987
Design   Steven R. Gilmore

Artiste   Tim Finn
Title   No Thunder No Fire No Rain
Rec Co   Virgin
Date   1986
Design   Caz Hildebrand; Photog David Hiscock

Artiste   Enya
Title   Watermark
Rec Co   WEA/Warner
Date   1988
Design   Laurence Dunmore; Photog David Hiscock

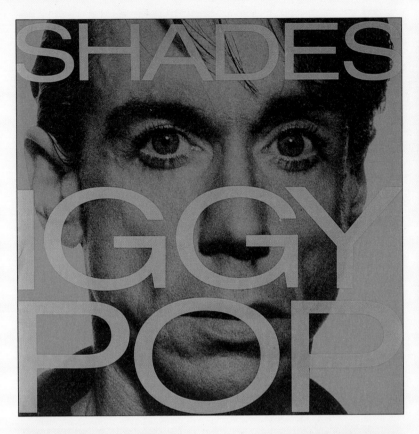

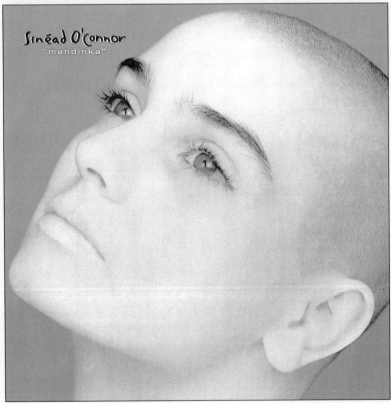

Artiste	Iggy Pop
Title	Shades
Rec Co	A & M
Date	1986
Design	Jeremy Pearce; Photog Robert Erdmann (courtesy The Face)

Artiste	Sinead O'Connor
Title	Mandinka
Rec Co	Ensign/Chrysalis
Date	1987
Design	Stephen Horse; Photog Mike Owen

Artiste	Bryan Ferry
Title	Limbo
Rec Co	Virgin
Date	1988
Design	Keith Breeden; Photog Albert Sanchez

Artiste	Miles Davis
Title	Tutu
Rec Co	Warner
Date	1986
Design	& Art Concept Eiko Ishioka; Photog Irving Penn

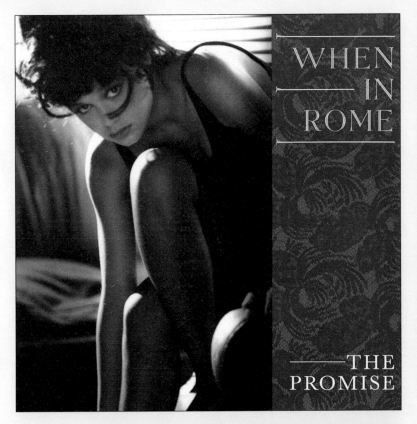

WHEN
IN
ROME

THE
PROMISE

Artiste   When in Rome
Title   The Promise
Rec Co   Ten/Virgin
Date   1988
Design   Proktor; Photog David Oldfield & James Martin

Artiste   Boy George
Title   Don't Cry (12″)
Rec Co   Virgin
Date   1988
Design   Mx & Tex at Assorted Images; Photog Industria/Brad Branson

Artiste   George Michael
Title   Faith
Rec Co   Epic/CBS
Date   1987
Design   Stylorouge/George Michael; Photog Russell Young

Artiste   Madonna
Title   True Blue
Rec Co   Sire/Warner
Date   1986
Design   Jeri McManus-Heiden

Artiste   Tanika Tikaram
Title   Ancient Heart
Rec Co   WEA/Warner
Date   1988
Design   T & CP

Artiste   The Leon Thomas Blues Band
Title   The Leon Thomas Blues Band
Rec Co   Portrait/CBS
Date   1988
Design   Photog Jonathon Postal; Lettering Bernie Maisner

Artiste   This Mortal Coil
Title   Come Here My Love
Rec Co   4AD
Date   1986
Design   Vaughan Oliver/23 envelope; Photog Nigel Grierson/23 envelope

Artiste   Annabel Lamb
Title   Brides
Rec Co   BMG/RCA
Date   1987
Design   Moira Bogue; Art Dir Michael Ross/Normal Service

Artiste   Kitaro
Title   Tenku
Rec Co   Geffen/Warner
Date   1986
Design   Art Dir Jeri McManus-Heiden; Photog Matt Mahurin

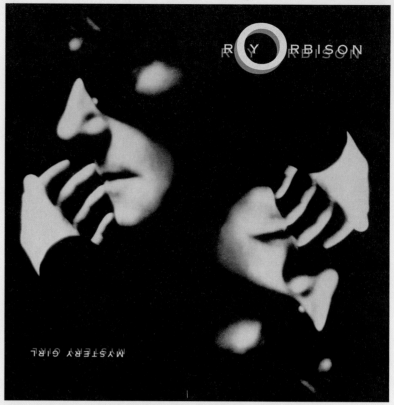

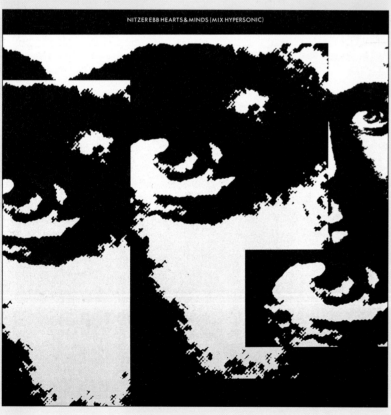

Artiste	Red Lorry Yellow Lorry
Title	Only Dreaming (Wide Awake)
Rec Co	Situation 2
Date	1988
Design	Photog Justin Thomas

Artiste	Nitzer Ebb
Title	Hearts and Minds
Rec Co	Mute Records
Date	1989
Design	Simon Grainger

Artiste	Roy Orbison
Title	Mystery Girl
Rec Co	Virgin
Date	1989
Design	Tim Stedman/Public Eye; Photog Glen Erler

Artiste	Cicone Youth
Title	The Whitey Album
Rec Co	Blast First/Mute
Date	1988
Design	Cicone Youth

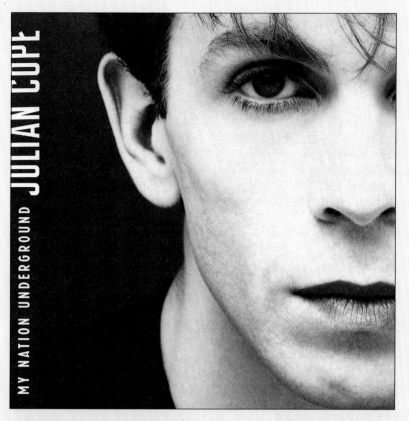

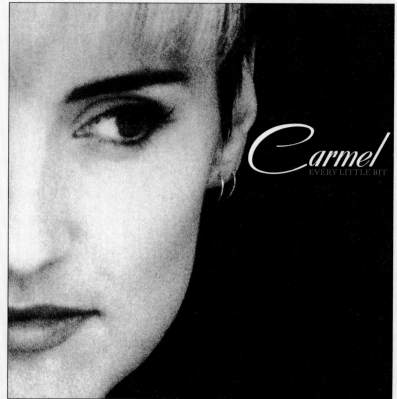

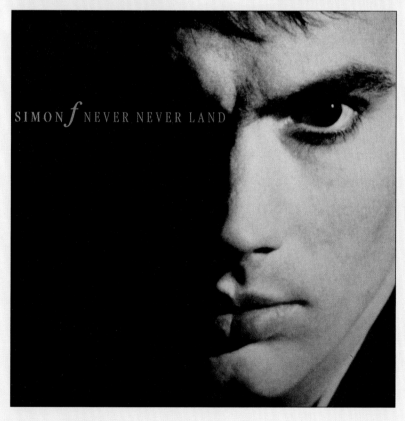

Artiste	Julian Cope
Title	My Nation Underground
Rec Co	Island
Date	1988
Design	Island Art; Photog Mike Owen

Artiste	Simon F
Title	Never Never Land
Rec Co	Reprise/Warner
Date	1987
Design	Jeri McManus-Heiden; Photog Paula Bullwinkle

Artiste	Carmel
Title	Every Little Bit
Rec Co	London
Date	1988
Design	DKB; Photog Frederique Veysset

Artiste	Roy Harper
Title	. . . Descendant of Smith
Rec Co	EMI
Date	1988
Design	Abrahams Pants; Photog Paul Cox

Artiste	Sade
Title	Turn My Back on You
Rec Co	Epic/CBS
Date	1988
Design	Graham Smith; Photog Matthew Rolston

Artiste	Brenda Russell
Title	Get Here
Rec Co	A & M
Date	1988
Design	Donald Krieger; Art Dir Chuck Beeson; Photog Raul Vega

Artiste	Sade
Title	Love is Stronger than Pride
Rec Co	Epic/CBS
Date	1988
Design	Sade, Graham Smith; Photog Levon Parian

Artiste	Enya
Title	Orinoco Flow (Sail Away)
Rec Co	WEA/Warner
Date	1988
Design	Laurence Dunmore; Photog Russell Young

Artiste   Prince
Title   Lovesexy
Rec Co   Paisley Park/Warner
Date   1988
Design   Photog Jean-Baptiste Mondino

Artiste   Siouxsie & The Banshees
Title   Peek-A-Boo
Rec Co   Polydor
Date   1988
Design   C-More-Tone Studios

Artiste   New Order
Title   Low-Life
Rec Co   Factory
Date   1988
Design   Peter Saville Assoc; Photog Trevor Key

Artiste   Danielle Dax
Title   Yummer Yummer Man
Rec Co   Awesome
Date   1985
Design   Artwork Holly Warburton

Artiste   Annie Pak
Title   Remix
Rec Co   Cinepoly
Date   1988
Design   Wally Lee; Photog Justin Chan

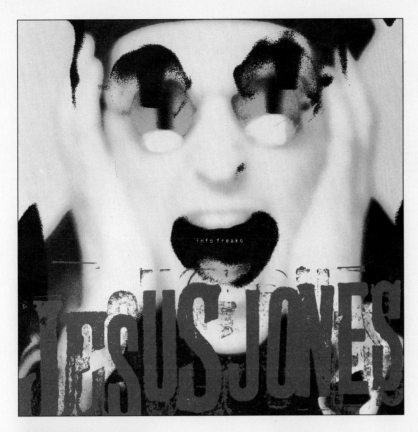

Artiste   Jesus H Jones
Title   Info Freako
Rec Co   Food
Date   1989
Design   Stylorouge; Photog Simon Fowler

Artiste   Oldland Montano
Title   Sugar Mummy
Rec Co   Siren/Virgin
Date   1987
Design   Michael Nash Assoc; Photog Andrew MacPherson

Artiste   Eurythmics
Title   Savage
Rec Co   RCA
Date   1987
Design   Laurence Stevens; Photog Alistair Thain

Artiste   Madonna
Title   Live To Tell
Rec Co   Sire/WEA
Date   1986
Design   Jeri McManus-Heiden; Photog Herb Ritts

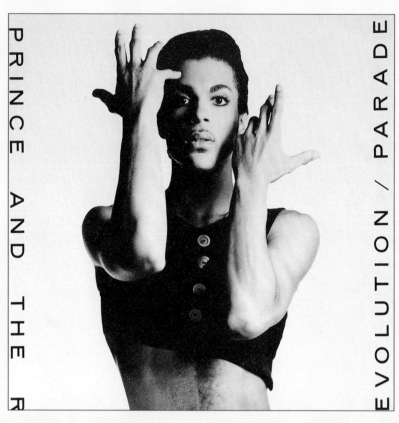

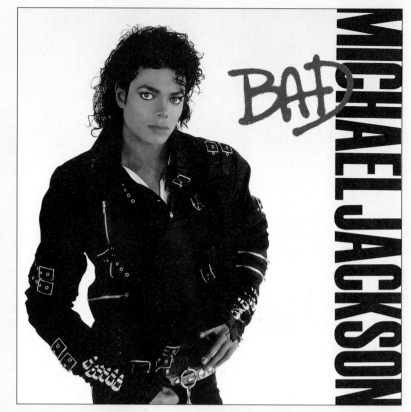

Artiste	Prince and the Revolution
Title	Parade
Rec Co	Warner
Date	1986
Design	Kim Champagne; Art Dir Laura LiPuma, Jeffrey Kent Ayeroff

Artiste	Habit
Title	Lucy (12″)
Rec Co	Virgin
Date	1988
Design	Mark Farrow/Three Assoc; Photog Sheila Rock

Artiste	Michael Jackson
Title	Bad
Rec Co	Epic/CBS
Date	1987
Design	Art Dir Tony Lane/Nancy Donald; Photog Sam Emerson; 'Bad' Lettering Jeffrey Spear

Artiste	Inxs
Title	Kick
Rec Co	Mercury/Phonogram
Date	1987
Design	& Art Dir Nick Egan asstd by Ken Smith & Bob Wither; Photog Grant Matthews

PART FOUR
PAINTINGS AND TEXTURES

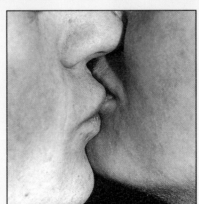

There are trends in album cover art as much as there are in other fields. Some are of course forgettable, but there are others to be applauded. Such is the case with a movement towards the more painterly or textural design. These are often related to mood and feeling rather than concept or image. They are sometimes low key and dimly lit. Often they are very minimal with the typography.

Look at page 117 for example or the frontispiece by Russell Mills. In both cases the lettering is very discreetly done, no longer is the name of the group in 6 ft high letters at the top of the album. Perhaps this tells us something about the band's attitude to packaging. They see it not purely as a selling device, but more an integral part of the music, part of the whole thing, to be explored in the same way as the music can be explored. A discerning public does not need a shattering image and slap-in-the-face graphics. Impact shmimpact.

Artiste   Siouxsie and the Banshees
Title   The Last Beat of my Heart
Rec Co   Polydor
Date   1988
Design   Sleeve Nigel Vichi/Banshees; Painting Kathy Ward; Photog Brian Udall

Artiste   Paul Rutherford
Title   Get Real
Rec Co   4th Broadway/Island
Date   1988
Design   Michael Nash Assoc

Artiste   All About Eve
Title   What Kind of Fool
Rec Co   Phonogram
Date   1988
Design   Stylorouge with All About Eve; Photog Avid Images;
           Portraits Simon Fowler/Andrew Catlin

Artiste   Miles Davis/Marcus Miller
Title   Music from Siesta
Rec Co   Warner
Date   1987
Design   Art Dir Deborah Norcross; Photog George Tooker

Artiste   Bruce Hornsby & The Range
Title   The Valley Road
Rec Co   RCA
Date   1988
Design   Photog Robert Llewelyn

heavenly
bodies

Artiste   Heavenly Bodies
Title   Celestial
Rec Co   Third Mind
Date   1988
Design   Artwork Dave Coppenhall

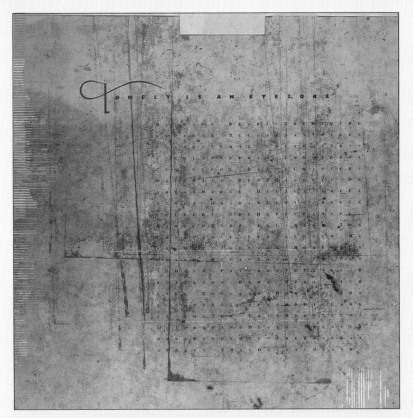

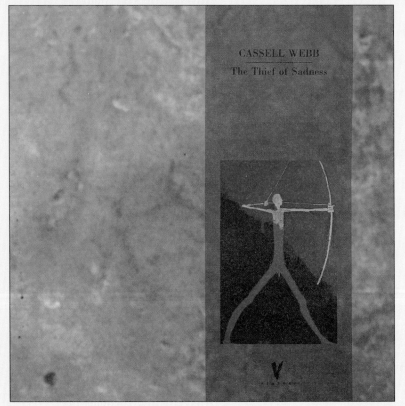

Artiste   Various
Title   Lonely is an Eyesore
Rec Co   4AD
Date   1987
Design   Vaughan Oliver/23 envelope

Artiste   Herb Robertson Quintet
Title   Live at Willisau "X-cerpts"
Rec Co   JMT Productions
Date   1987
Design   Thom Argauer; Art Steve Byram

Artiste   What is This
Title   What is This
Rec Co   MCA
Date   1985
Design   & Photog Glen Wexler, Jeff Adamoff; Design concept
           Michael F Lawrence

Artiste   Cassell Webb
Title   The Thief of Sadness
Rec Co   Venture
Date   1987
Design   Icon; Artwork Mekon

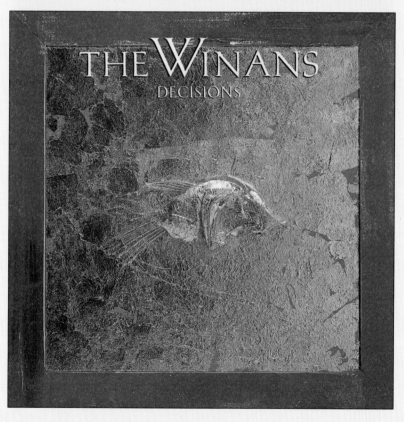

Artiste   Ennio Morricone
Title   Film Music 1966-87
Rec Co   Virgin
Date   1987
Design   Art Dir Andrew W Ellis/Gary Wathen

Artiste   The Winans
Title   Decisions
Rec Co   Qwest/Warner
Date   1987
Design   Mary Ann Dibbs

Artiste   Luxuria Devoto Noko
Title   Public Highway/Shortcut
Rec Co   Beggars Banquet
Date
Design   Christopher Bigg

Artiste   Roy Orbison
Title   You got It
Rec Co   Virgin
Date   1989
Design   Tim Stedman/Mac James/Public Eye; Photog Glen Eriex

Artiste	Throwing Muses
Title	The Fat Skier
Rec Co	4AD
Date	1987
Design	Art Dir Kurt De Munbrun; Photog Richard Donelly & Kate Whitney

Artiste	Yellowjackets
Title	Politics
Rec Co	MCA
Date	1988
Design	Art Dir Jeff Lancaster/L-Shape; Illus Lou Beach; Photog Aaron Rappaport

Artiste	Graham Parker
Title	The Mona Lisa's Sister
Rec Co	RCA/BMG
Date	1988
Design	Laurence Stevens; Photog Jolie Parker

Artiste	The Cure
Title	Catch (12″)
Rec Co	Fiction
Date	1987
Design	Parched Art/Andy Vella, Porl Thompson

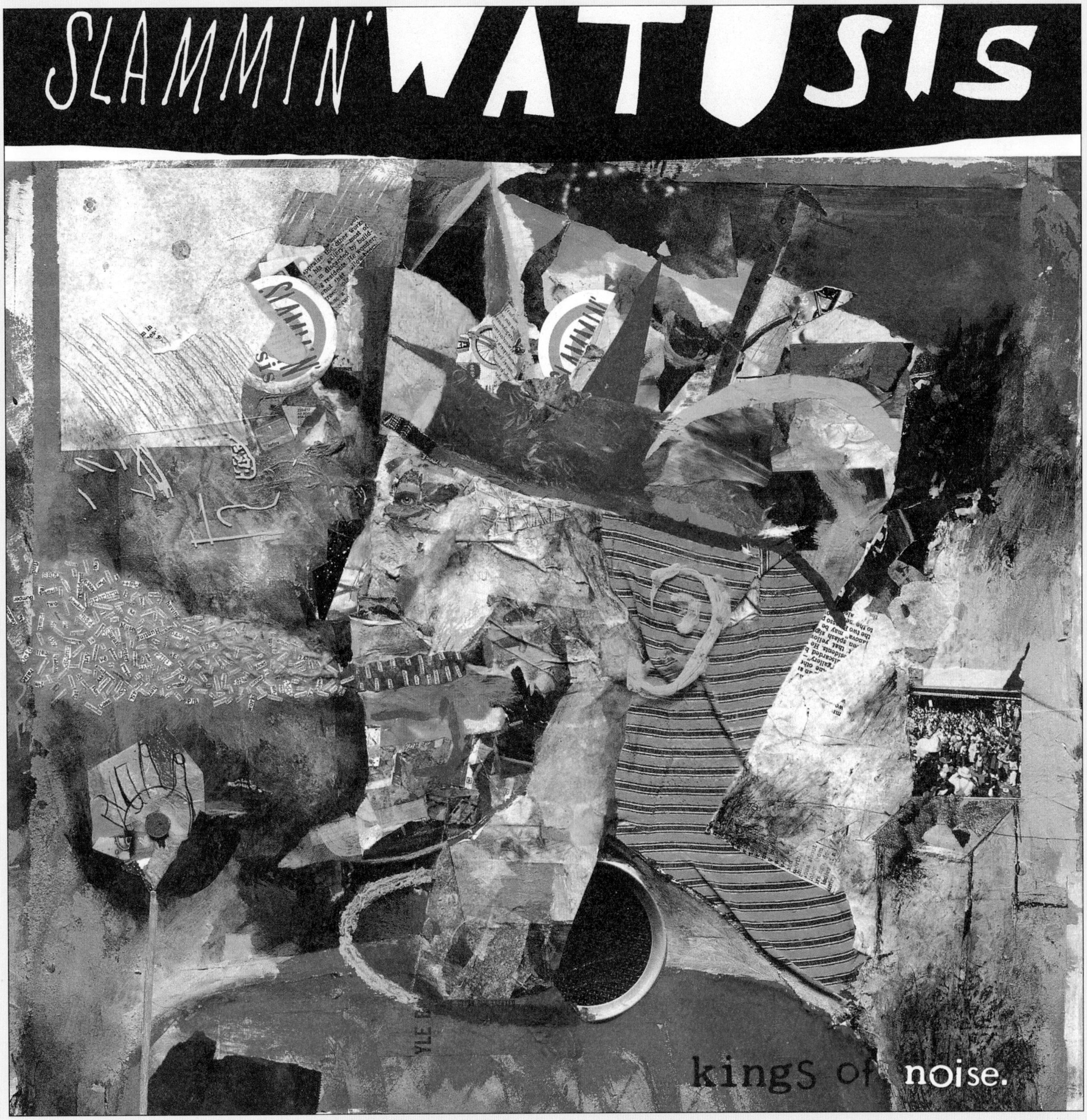

Artiste   Slammin' Watusis
Title   Kings of Noise
Rec Co   Epic
Date   1989
Design   & Cover Art Steve Byram; Photog Tony Soluri

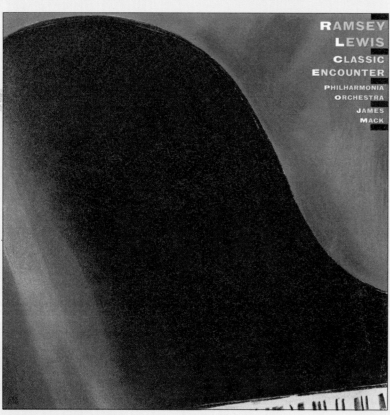

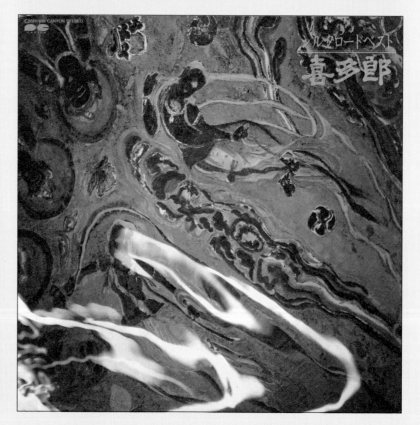

Artiste	Harold Budd
Title	Lovely Thunder
Rec Co	EG/Opal
Date	1986
Design	& Art Russell Mills; Design Assist Dave Coppenhall; Photog David Buckland

Artiste	Ramsey Lewis-Philharmonia Orchestra & James Mack
Title	Classic Encounter
Rec Co	CBS
Date	1988
Design	Art Dir Christopher Austopchuk; Illus Vivienne Flesher

Artiste	Danielle Dax
Title	Cat-House
Rec Co	Awesome
Date	1988
Design	Photog Holly Warburton

Artiste	Kitaro
Title	Silk Road Vests
Rec Co	Canyon — Japan
Date	—
Design	—

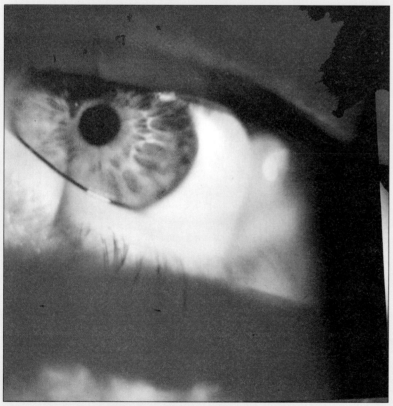

Artiste	Felt
Title	Poem of the River
Rec Co	Creation
Date	1987
Design	Photog Sandy Fleming; Artwork Shanghai Packaging Co.

Artiste	The Cure
Title	Kiss Me Kiss Me Kiss Me
Rec Co	Fiction
Date	1987
Design	Parched Art/Andy Vella, Porl Thompson

Artiste	Mick Karn
Title	Dreams of Reason Produce Monsters
Rec Co	Virgin
Date	1987
Design	Photog Richard Haughton

Artiste	That Petrol Emotion
Title	Manic Pop Thrill
Rec Co	Demon
Date	1986
Design	& Photog Hugh Cairns; Typography Mike Krage

Artiste   Was (Not Was)
Title   What Up, Dog?
Rec Co   Fontana/Phonogram
Date   1987
Design   Art Dir Jon & Vicky/The Unknown Partnership; Illus Christoph Simon
           & Karen Kelly for Pankino

Artiste   Heart
Title   Bad Animals
Rec Co   Capitol/EMI
Date   1987
Design   & Art Dir Norman Moore; Photog Phillip Dixon

Artiste   Ahmad Jamal
Title   Poinciana
Rec Co   Portrait/CBS
Date   1989
Design   Art Stephen Kronnenger; Art Dir Steve Byram

Artiste   Motian
Title   Monk in Motian
Rec Co   JMT/Polydor
Date   1988
Design   & Art Steve Byram

Artiste   Throwing Muses
Title   House Tornado
Rec Co   4AD
Date   1987
Design   & Art Dir Vaughan Oliver/v23; Painting Shinro Ohtake

Artiste	Dinosaur JR
Title	Bug
Rec Co	Blast First
Date	1988
Design	Maura Jasper

Artiste	Toni Childs
Title	Union
Rec Co	A & M
Date	1988
Design	Art Dir Chuck Beeson/Melanie Nissen; Painting John Howard

Artiste	Steve Tilston
Title	Life by Misadventure
Rec Co	Run River
Date	1987
Design	& Photog Gary Marsh; Front Cover Photo Allan Tipping

Artiste	Paris Saxophone Quartet
Title	JS Bach
Rec Co	CBS
Date	1985
Design	Josephine DiDonato; Illus Jeff Dodson

Artiste   Los Lobos
Title   La Pistola y El Corazon
Rec Co   Slash/Warner
Date   1988
Design   Jeri McManus-Heiden

Artiste	Hugo Largo
Title	Turtle Song
Rec Co	Land
Date	1989
Design	Dave Coppenhall

Artiste	Heavenly Bodies
Title	Rains on Me
Rec Co	Third Mind
Date	1988
Design	Dave Coppenhall

Artiste	Ginger Baker
Title	Horses & Trees
Rec Co	Celluloid
Date	1986
Design	Thi Linh Le Painting Shinro Ohtake (1986)

Artiste	Lone Justice
Title	Shelter
Rec Co	Geffen
Date	1986
Design	Kim Champagne; Cover Cooper Edens

Artiste   Harold Budd, Elizabeth Fraser, Robin Guthrie, Simon Raymonde
Title   The Moon and the Melodies
Rec Co   4AD
Date   1986
Design   Vaughan Oliver/23 envelope; Photog Nigel Grierson/23 envelope

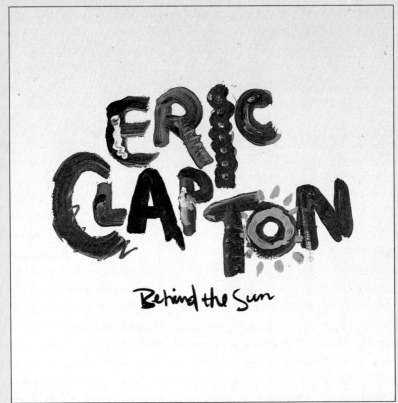

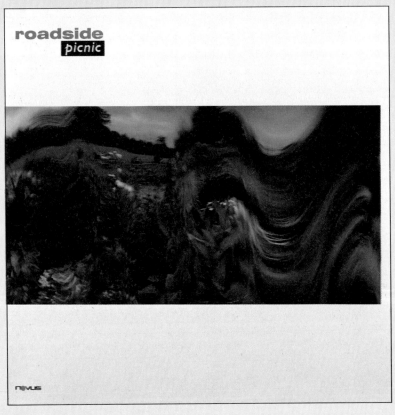

Artiste   Chris McGregor Brotherhood of Breath
Title   Country Cooking
Rec Co   Venture/Warner
Design   Icon; Artwork Mekon; Photog Andrew W. Ellis

Artiste   Roadside Picnic
Title   Roadside Picnic
Rec Co   Novus/BMG
Date   1988
Design   The Leisure Process; Photog Jim Friedman

Artiste   Eric Clapton
Title   Behind the Sun
Rec Co   Duck/Warner
Date   1983
Design   & Art Dir/Painting Larry Vigon; Photog Patti Clapton

Artiste   Penguin Cafe Orchestra
Title   When in Rome...
Rec Co   EG
Date   1988
Design   Bill Smith Studio; Painting Emily Young; Photog Patrizia Giancotti

PART FIVE
DESIGN CONTINUITY

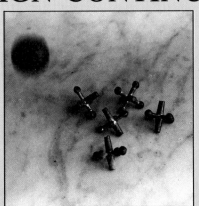

Many designers, such as Keith Breeden and John Warwicker, believe that the entire packaging, including back cover, booklet or inner sleeve label and single bags, logos and advertising, should be strongly integrated — they should all relate visually and thematically. This 'design continuity' may span one project, or several projects (Scritti Politti), or a record series (pages 125-6).

There are numerous arguments in favour of this thesis and equally numerous solutions to support it, ranging from those that are only loosely connected to those that develop, redefine and expand specific graphic or pictorial content. We have touched upon it only briefly here but will devote a much larger section of *ACA 6* to the same subject. It obviously makes sense, but hopefully only as a predilection, not as a rule. Rock 'n' roll don't need rules.

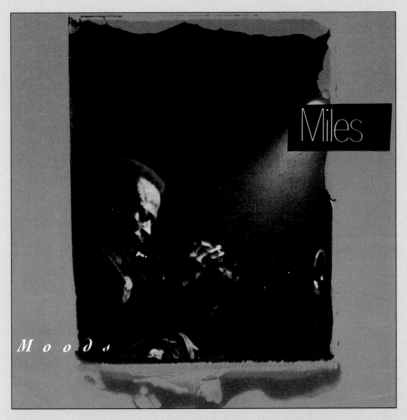

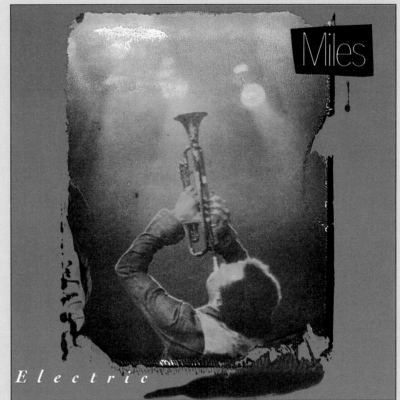

Artiste	Miles Davis
Title	Moods
Rec Co	CBS
Date	1988
Design	Christopher Austopchuk

Artiste	Miles Davis
Title	Blues
Rec Co	CBS
Date	1988
Design	Christopher Austopchuk

Artiste	Miles Davis
Title	Electric
Rec Co	CBS
Date	1988
Design	Christopher Austopchuk

Artiste	Miles Davis
Title	Standards
Rec Co	CBS
Date	1988
Design	Christopher Austopchuk

Artiste   Eduardo Niebla/Antonio Forcione
Title   Celebration
Rec Co   Venture
Date   1987
Design   Icon; Illus Richard Evans; Artwork Mekon

Artiste   Peter de Havilland
Title   Bois de Boulogne
Rec Co   Venture
Date   1987
Design   Icon; Photog Richard Evans; Artwork Mekon

Artiste   Hans-Joachim Roedelius
Title   Momenti Felici
Rec Co   Venture
Date   1987
Design   Icon; Photog Roedelius; Artwork Mekon

Artiste   Lester Bowie's Brass Fantasy
Title   Twilight Dreams
Rec Co   Venture
Date   1987
Design   Icon; Photog Andrew Ellis; Artwork Mekon

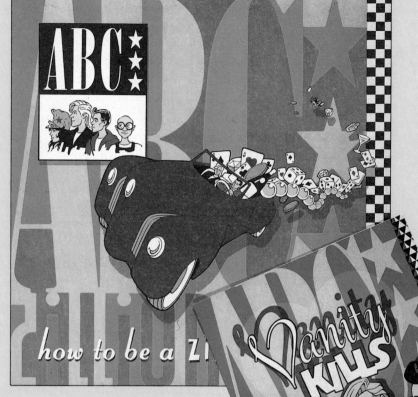

Artiste   ABC
Title   How to be a Zillionaire
Rec Co   Phonogram
Date   1985
Design   Keith Breeden/Design KB

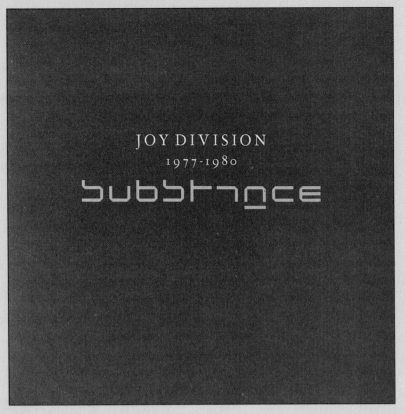

JOY DIVISION
1977-1980
subsɬɒnce

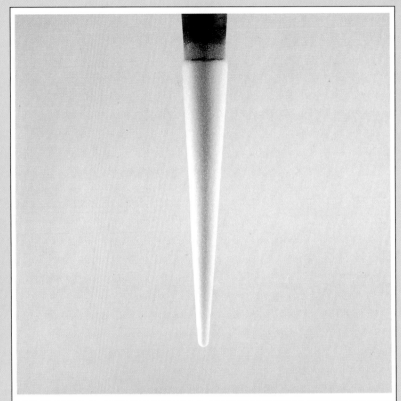

JOY DIVISION
1979
ɒɬmosphere

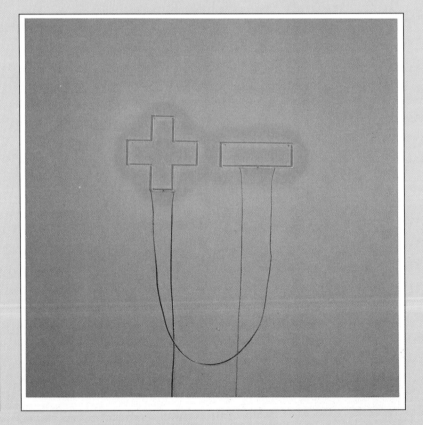

Artiste	Joy Division
Title	Substance
Rec Co	Factory Communications Ltd
Date	1988
Design	Peter Saville Assoc

Artiste	Joy Division
Title	Atmosphere
Rec Co	Factory Communications Ltd
Date	1988
Design	Peter Saville Assoc

Artiste	Joy Division
Title	Substance (liner bag)
Rec Co	Factory Communications Ltd
Date	1988
Design	Art Dir Peter Saville Assoc; Sculpture Energie Piek Ijs, detail by Jan Van Munster 1981; Photog Trevor Key

Artiste	Joy Division
Title	Atmosphere (liner bag)
Rec Co	Factory Communications Ltd
Date	1988
Design	Art Dir Peter Saville Assoc; Sculpture Plus en Min, detail by Jan Van Munster 1986; Photog Trevor Key

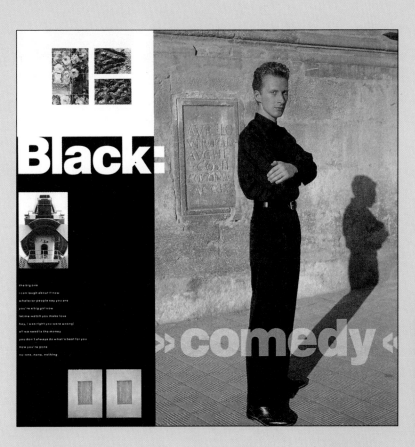

Artiste	Black
Title	Comedy
Rec Co	A & M
Date	1988
Design	John Warwicker/Jeremy Pearce; Photog Perry Ogden

Artiste	Black
Title	You're a Big Girl Now
Rec Co	A & M
Date	1988
Design	John Warwicker/Jeremy Pearce; Photog Perry Ogden

Artiste	Black
Title	Comedy
Rec Co	A & M
Date	1988
Design	John Warwicker/Jeremy Pearce; Photog Perry Ogden

Artiste	Black
Title	The Big One
Rec Co	A & M
Date	1988
Design	John Warwicker/Jeremy Pearce; Photog Perry Ogden

Artiste   Ellis Beggs & Howard
Title   Where did Tomorrow Go?
Rec Co   BMG/RCA
Date   1988
Design   Storm Thorgerson/Keith Breeden; Photog Andy Earl

Artiste   Ellis Beggs & Howard
Title   Big Bubbles No Troubles
Rec Co   BMG/RCA
Date   1988
Design   Storm Thorgerson/Keith Breeden; Photog Andy Earl

Artiste   Ellis Beggs & Howard
Title   Homelands
Rec Co   BMG/RCA
Date   1988
Design   Storm Thorgerson/Keith Breeden; Photog Andy Earl/Tony May

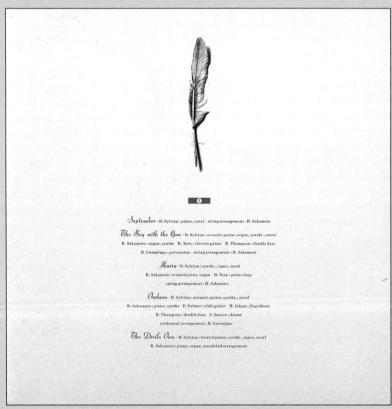

Artiste   David Sylvian
Title   Secrets of the Beehive
Rec Co   Virgin
Date   1987
Design   Vaughan Oliver/23 envelope; Photog Nigel Grierson/23 envelope

Artiste   David Sylvian
Title   Secrets of the Beehive (sleeve notes)
Rec Co   Virgin
Date   1987
Design   Vaughan Oliver/23 envelope; Photog Nigel Grierson/23 envelope

Artiste   David Sylvian
Title   Let the Happiness In
Rec Co   Virgin
Date   1987
Design   Vaughan Oliver/23 envelope; Photog Nigel Grierson/23 envelope

Artiste   David Sylvian
Title   Orpheus
Rec Co   Virgin
Date   1988
Design   & typography Vaughan Oliver/23 envelope; Photog Nigel Grierson/
           23 envelope

Artiste   David Sylvian
Title   Secrets of the Beehive
Rec Co   Virgin
Date   1987
Design   Photog Nigel Grierson/23 envelope

FIRST BOY IN THIS TOWN
(Lovesick)...........................

Includes Limited Edition Colour Prints of 'Wood Beez', 'Absolute' and 'Hypnotize' Sleeves.

WOOD BEEZ

(PRAY LIKE ARETHA FRANKLIN)

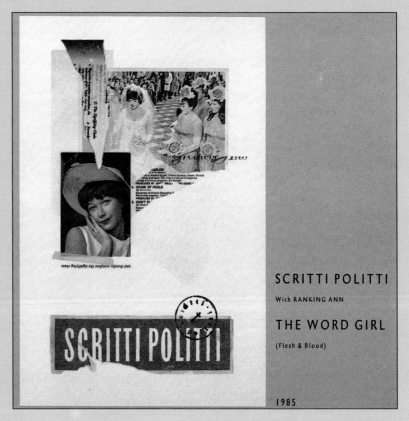

SCRITTI POLITTI

With RANKING ANN

THE WORD GIRL

(Flesh & Blood)

1985

Artiste	Scritti Politti
Title	First Boy in this Town
Rec Co	Virgin
Date	1988
Design	Keith Breeden/Green

Artiste	Scritti Politti
Title	Provision
Rec Co	Warner
Date	1988
Design	Keith Breeden/Green; Photog Jurgen Teller

Artiste	Scritti Politti
Title	Wood Beez
Rec Co	Virgin
Date	1983
Design	Keith Breeden/Green

Artiste	Scritti Politti with Ranking Ann
Title	The Word Girl
Rec Co	Virgin
Date	1985
Design	Keith Breeden/Green

Artiste   Scritti Politti
Title   Absolute
Rec Co   Virgin
Date   1984
Design   Caryn Gough/Keith Breeden/Green

136

Artiste   Young MC, Def Jef, Tone Lōc, Body and Soul, G Love E
Title   Eat to the Beat Delicious Vinyl
Rec Co   Island/4th Broadway
Date   1989
Design   Michael Nash Assoc

INDEX

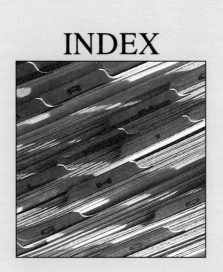

INDEX

140

ROGER DEAN

Roger Dean was born in Kent, England, in 1944. He studied industrial design at Canterbury College of Art from 1961 to 1965, and then went on to study in the Furniture School at the Royal College of Art, graduating in 1968 with a Masters degree in Design.

Then, as now, his first concern was with three-dimensional design, but in 1968, while working on the seating he had designed for the "Upstairs" room at Ronnie Scott's jazz club in London, he was commissioned to design his first album cover for a group called Gun. Since then he has illustrated over sixty album covers for such bands as Yes, Uriah Heep, Osibisa, Greenslade and Asia.

In 1975 the first collection of his work, the book "Views" was published and in 1984 Roger and Martyn Dean published "Magnetic Storm", the sequel to "Views". Currently he is working on the design of various resort projects around the world and designing houses to be built in California.

STORM THORGERSON

Born, if that's the word, in Potters Bar, Middlesex 1944. Moved through Grays in Essex and Whitley Bay in Northumberland and settled in Cambridge. Schooled, if that's also the word, at A.S. Neill's Summerhill, the original free school, Brunswick Primary and Cambs High School.

Disturbed early years were followed by exciting teenage life in early 60s, in Cambridge from which emerged several artistes and musicians including Pink Floyd. Adolescence blighted only by parents' divorce.

Dedicated student for six years reading English at Leicester University (BA) and then studying film and TV at Royal College of Art in London (MA). Began Hipgnosis with Aubrey Powell (Po) 1968 more by chance than anything, and ended up designing album covers for Pink Floyd, Led Zeppelin, Genesis and many others.

Turned to videos in 1983 by forming Green Back Films with Po and Peter Christopherson, and making clips for Paul Young, Yes, Robert Plant, Nik Kershaw, before disbanding in 1985 due to severe financial difficulties. Later joined PMI, Harry Films and Lee Lacy and has been making films ever since, plus the occasional record cover and book.

NIGEL GRIERSON

Nigel Grierson was born in Fishburn, County Durham in 1959. After Newcastle-Upon-Tyne Poly, he gained an MA in Photography from the Royal College of Art in 1980 and an MA in Film in 1982.

Nigel is one half of the photography design partnership known as 23 Envelope. His intensely personal photographic style has become particularly synonymous with the independent record label 4AD. Responding to the mood and atmosphere of the music, he has emerged with images rich in texture that work away from the literalness inherent in the photographic image.

Since 1986 he has divided his time between designing record sleeves and directing music videos (Black, David Sylvian, Clannad) under the umbrella of the production company HLA.

He is presently developing ideas for long format video projects with David Sylvian and Harold Budd. He lives in a power station in Greenwich.